Blanchot and Literary Criticism

Blanchot and Literary Criticism

Mark Hewson

continuum

The Continuum International Publishing Group
The Tower Building, 11 York Road, London SE1 7NX
80 Maiden Lane, New York, NY 10038

www.continuumbooks.com

© 2011 Mark Hewson

All rights reserved. No part of this book may be reproduced, stored in a retrieval system, or transmitted, in any form or by any means, electronic, mechanical, photocopying, recording, or otherwise, without the permission of the publishers.

Excerpts from "Literature and the right to death" in *The Station Hill Blanchot Reader* by Maurice Blanchot, translated by Lydia Davis, Paul Auster and Robert Lamberton, edited by George Quasha, reproduced by permission of Station Hill Press. © 1998 Station Hill/Barrytown Ltd. All rights reserved.

Excerpt from *The Space of Literature* by Maurice Blanchot, translated by Ann Smock, reproduced by permisson of the University of Nebraska Press. Copyright © 1955 Editions Gallimard. © 1982 University of Nebraska. All rights reserved.

Excerpts from *The Work of Fire* by Maurice Blanchot, translated by Charlotte Mandell, reproduced by permission of Stanford University Press. © 1995 Board of Trustees of the Leland Stanford Jr. University. All rights reserved.

Library of Congress Cataloging-in-Publication Data
Hewson, Mark.
Blanchot and literary criticism / Mark Hewson.
   p. cm.
Includes bibliographical references and index.
ISBN 978-0-8264-2461-7 (hardback : alk. paper) — ISBN 978-1-4411-1523-2 (pbk. : alk. paper) 1. Blanchot, Maurice–Criticism and interpretation. 2. Blanchot, Maurice—Philosophy. 3. Literature—History and criticism—Theory, etc. 4. Literature—Philosophy. I. Title.
PQ2603.L3343Z6756 2011
801'.95092—dc22   2011007240

ISBN: 9780826424617 (hardcover)
            9781441115232 (paperback)

Typeset by Newgen Imaging Systems Pvt Ltd, Chennai, India

Contents

Abbreviations vii
Introduction: Blanchot and Literary Criticism viii

1 The Modern Age and the 'Work' of Literature   1
2 Poetic Solitude: Two Essays on Hölderlin   21
3 Mallarmé and Modern Poetics   37
4 The Ambiguity of the Negative   66
5 Myth and Representation in Blanchot's Literary Criticism 103

Reprise: Blanchot and Literary Criticism   136

Selected Bibliography   143
Index   149

Abbreviations

The following abbreviations will be used for frequently cited works. Page numbers will be cited with these abbreviations, with the first number in each case referring to the original French, and the second to the English translations. The editions used are listed in the bibliography.

FP *Faux pas* (1943): translated as *Faux Pas*. Trans. Charlotte Mandell. Stanford: Stanford UP, 2001.
PF *La Part du feu* (1949): translated as *The Work of Fire*. Trans. Charlotte Mandell. Stanford: Stanford UP, 1995.
EL *L'Espace littéraire* (1955): translated as *The Space of Literature*. Trans. Anne Smock. Lincoln: University of Nebraska Press, 1982.
LV *Le Livre à venir* (1959): translated as *The Book to Come*. Trans. Charlotte Mandell. Stanford: Stanford UP, 2003.
EI *L'Entretien infini* (1969): translated as *The Infinite Conversation*. Trans. Susan Hanson. Minneapolis: University of Minnesota Press, 1993.
A *L'Amitié* (1971): translated as *Friendship*. Trans. Elizabeth Rottenberg. Stanford: Stanford UP, 1997.

Introduction: Blanchot and Literary Criticism

Maurice Blanchot's writings on literature have imposed themselves within the canon and syllabi of modern poetics and literary theory, and yet maintained a somewhat mysterious presence, rarely being invoked or contested in the methodological and ideological debates of literary studies and theory. There has not emerged a sense of a position or a tendency represented by his work, and even in the case of *L'Espace littéraire*, often represented in anthologies and histories of modern poetics/literary theory, the actual influence exercised by the work has remained a matter of isolated themes. 'The Two Versions of the Imaginary', for example, is often cited in discussions of the concept of the image, in art history and psychoanalytic criticism, and the texts on the *récit* (such as 'The Encounter with the Imaginary' and 'The Narrative Voice') appear in discussion of narrative genres. But these impulses, as productive as they may be, are confined by their context to a specific topic, and therefore do not necessarily pose the question as to where Blanchot's work stands in relation to criticism more generally – that is, how their ambiguous relation to the field of literary criticism should be conceptualized, and what limitations their exteriority place upon their appropriation or their contestation by literary critics.

These questions must, however, be addressed by a study devoted specifically to Blanchot's 'critical' writings. In beginning to read works such as *La Part du feu* (1949) *L'Espace littéraire* (1955) or *Le Livre à venir* (1959), one naturally assumes that they are generically located within the domain of criticism. The majority of the essays in these books are studies of individual authors, while others deal with literary historical questions, or with literary genre concepts. And yet the language and the kinds of claims made in these essays are at times so difficult to reconcile with the discourse of criticism that one comes to wonder if the initial identification is not misleading. This problem can be explained to some extent by the institutional context. Blanchot's essays were regularly published in journals such

Introduction: Blanchot and Literary Criticism   ix

as *Critique*, *Les Temps modernes* and *La Nouvelle Revue française* (NRF), where a serious discussion of literature, philosophy and politics was maintained outside the university context, something that is today very rare. Although obviously aware of scholarly tradition, such work is not subject to the various formal procedures by which, under the imperatives of organized research and pedagogy, knowledge is legitimated and consequently comes to assume a consistent 'style' at the level of methodology, structure and discourse. This situation is only a partial explanation, however. Blanchot's earliest essays, collected in *Faux Pas* (1943), clearly belong to such an autonomous tradition of criticism, typically located in a more public, cultural forum such as the literary periodical, and based around the review of a recently published work rather than the 'study' of a given text or historical or theoretical issue. From *La Part du feu* (1949) onwards, there is a visible tendency to deviate from the review format, although some attempt is made at preserving its outer appearance: this appears to be the result of the greater latitude Blanchot was granted in his contributions, in function of the increased recognition of his work.[1] The result is a mode of writing that is in some respects actually closer to literary studies in the disciplinary sense. No longer tied to the circumstances of the review, the essays can deal in greater detail with the literary production of a single author, typically ranging freely over the whole corpus. Although the texts of *La Part du feu* are not published within an academic context, the very project of a total study of individual authors and works seems to suppose the emergence of the norms of scholarship and research into the literary field, alongside the more traditional critical essay, oriented towards evaluation and appreciation. This does not, however, necessarily mean that the critical task is conceived in the same way as in the discipline of literary studies. In his essay on Blanchot in *Blindness and Insight*, Paul de Man writes:

> When we read [Blanchot] on one of the poets or novelists he happens to choose for a theme, we readily forget all we assumed to know up till then about this writer. This does not happen

---

1   On Blanchot's career and the publishing context, the best source of information is Christophe Bident's excellent biographical study, *Maurice Blanchot: Partenaire Invisible*. Paris: Champ Vallon, 1998.

because Blanchot's insight necessarily compels us to modify our perspective: this is by no means always the case. Returning afterwards to the author in question, we will find ourselves back at the same point, our understanding barely enriched by the comments of the critic. Blanchot, in fact, never intended to perform a task of exegesis that would combine earlier acquired knowledge with new elucidations.[2]

Even if the critical content is more considerable than de Man's remarks here allow – as this study will suggest – one cannot begin to place it in relation to literary studies without taking account of all that separates it from this field.

It is significant that the 'task of exegesis' is conceived by de Man in terms that bring it very close to the model of the sciences (taking this term in the wider sense). It is understood as an ongoing and collective process of research, with established authorities that can be invoked or contested and the prospect of an increase of knowledge or a more synthetic understanding over time. The more traditional kind of criticism, while it does not originate within this 'scientific' institutional structure, is not at all incompatible with the kinds of interpretation produced by literary studies as an academic discipline. It is assumed that the understanding contained in traditional criticism can in principle be separated out from its essayistic and rhetorical framework. A critical argument will often develop in dialectical engagement with a thesis from the reception history, which can be either scholarly or critical. Blanchot's essays, however, pose obstacles to this process of integration that are more fundamental, and that cannot be overcome merely by condensing and summarizing. These difficulties are manifest first of all in a certain practice of language. Although Blanchot's writing retains some of the 'classical' qualities of the literary essay, it also has many distinctive and unusual features, and innovations appear in each phase of his production. These become fully apparent from *L'Espace littéraire* (1955), where we see a further modification of the critical mode. This work, like *La Part du feu*, is made up of extended essays on particular writers – Mallarmé, Kafka, Rilke and Hölderlin – but these studies are presented as part of

---

2 *Blindness and Insight: Essays in the Rhetoric of Contemporary Criticism*. Minneapolis: University of Minnesota Press, 1983, 62.

an integrated meditation on the demand that the literary work makes upon its writer and its reader, and a narrative and dramatic description of the act of writing as an experience of 'the night', of solitude and the absence of time. This meditation belongs to no immediately recognizable genre or discourse. The conclusions are framed in a language that is proper to this text alone: the literary work is the site of 'communication', in which 'the obscure makes itself light', in which 'dissimulation becomes appearance' (EL 265, 199); literature is the experience of 'dispersion' (LV 279, 205), of 'neutrality' (LV 285, 209); to write is 'to hold oneself [. . .] in relation to the Neuter' (EI 384, 256).

If one considers such claims in the context of literary criticism – including the various forms of theoretically inspired literary criticism – then I think it must be said that this language does not have the character of conceptual generality that could allow it to be used in research and teaching, for the description or conceptualization of literary and cultural phenomena. The language is 'hermetic' in the sense that, far from being a generally available instrument, subject to modification by an ongoing collective work of inquiry, its meaning is inseparably linked to its deployment in the texts, and in particular, to the technique of repetition and variation of terms that Blanchot exercises with such mastery. This should not, however lead to the conclusion that we have here to do with a 'poetic' language, a language that would be evocative and mysterious, without precise meaning. On the contrary, as I will show in later parts of this study, Blanchot's 'hermetic' language condenses and articulates a philosophical thought that maintains itself at a distance in principle from the cognitive project of the sciences (in the wider sense), and that claims to deal with questions that cannot appear within such inquiry, but that are nonetheless implicated in its foundations.

The thought is not, however, developed in the context of a philosophical teaching; this is the point at which the institutional location of Blanchot is really significant, and which separates his work from that of related thinkers such as Heidegger or Levinas, or even Sartre whose philosophy is presented in the mode of a teaching, although he did not actually occupy a university post.[3] Blanchot's thought has

---

3   Blanchot considers the form of philosophical exposition and its relation to teaching in an essay entitled 'Thought and the Demand of Discontinuity', in *L'Entretien infini* (I.i).

its institutional and discursive framework in the practice of literary criticism, a situation his work occupies between 1940 and 1960 (after which the 'critical' element tends to recede significantly, despite occasional essays still appearing on literary writers and topics). One can say, then, that criticism here provides the format and the medium within which a philosophical thought develops. This would account for the freedom of Blanchot's work in relation to the imperatives of the form it chooses, preserving such aspects as serve the interest of its movement and dispensing with those it does not. And in this sense, it is clearly significant that in the course of his work, literary studies comes to play a lesser role, and that in *L'Entretien infini* (1969), the philosophical thought becomes more directly the focus.

What is important in this context, however, is that as a result of its initial institutional location, Blanchot's work does contain the essential elements of criticism as an intellectual enterprise, and even as a form of research: it has its corpus of texts, its critical problem, and a practice of reading that is guided by the problem posed. The question of Blanchot's relation to literary criticism, then, gives an angle of approach to his work that, while clearly authorized by the texts, is nonetheless external to their own rhetoric and movement. It allows a certain distance and perspective upon texts which, due to their unique force and assurance, make it very difficult at once to take them on their own terms and to maintain a detached and critical attitude. The practice of literary criticism, as we will see, is something more for Blanchot than a neutral medium that is merely 'occupied' for other purposes. The philosophical thought is initially developed as part of an interpretation of a literary phenomenon, and this path should not be assumed to be merely incidental. On the contrary, the claim is that the significance of the literary phenomenon in question cannot be recognized within the limits of the discipline, and that it demands the inclusion of orders of consideration that would not normally fall under its responsibility.

This study does not attempt to provide an overview of Blanchot's critical work as a whole. Instead, it examines in detail a sequence of quite narrowly defined areas of Blanchot's production. Each of the chapters deals with a small number of texts that are closely related in terms of either their topic or the thought that they develop. This approach corresponds to something in the composition of Blanchot's work, which tends to be distributed in 'clusters' of varying dimensions – groups of essays dealing with similar topics, or with clear thematic or linguistic links. In order to see the critical problem that is at the centre of the work we begin with a set of texts written in the late 1940s and early 1950s. This location is significant since it corresponds to another shift in Blanchot's critical practice, concomitant with the introduction of the language of 'the outside'. Up to and including *La Part du feu* (1949), Blanchot's books give the impression of being collections of relatively discrete essays; the subjects appear to have been chosen according to the occasion of their initial journal publication or to personal interest. At this point, however, the work as a whole comes into a different light, with the introduction of a historical standpoint, from which it becomes possible to conceive most if not all the writers studied as belonging to one historical phenomenon. In these essays, Blanchot positions his studies within a philosophical–historical interpretation of modernity, derived from a free adaptation of Hegel and Heidegger, and inflected by the French reception of Hegel in writers such as Sartre, Kojève and Hyppolite. The situation of modern literature is defined by its encounter with the great clarification represented by the modern conceptions of historical freedom and rationality, and with the liquidation of all the doctrines and values by which art and writing could be granted an exceptional status. For art and literature, Blanchot suggests, the modern epoch signifies a kind of legitimation-crisis, a privation of the privileges and expectations transmitted with the literary tradition. The question of the meaning and value of art – or the implication that it is not so very great – is contained in the positive decisions by which modern reason and modern society re-define and consolidate themselves. It follows that literary production, henceforth, will be mediated by the question of what it means that poetry and literature exist at all. For Blanchot, however, the result of this interrogation is not necessarily an effort at self-justification, nor does it only produce the anxiety and the self-doubt that comes from the sense of being without an assigned place in the scheme of things. If modern literature can claim to be a new departure, it is inasmuch as it able to appropriate and mobilize the question of its own existence: all the great modern works, Blanchot writes, have 'their own possibility as their centre' (LV 169, 123).

The historical formation that Blanchot makes visible is therefore not circumscribed by specific national contexts and literary movements and periods; it is most concentrated in certain key figures, such as Mallarmé, or Hölderlin, but is also present in many other writers who do not have direct similarities or affiliations at the level of style or ideas. One cannot say that the essays devoted to the individual writers treated in the volumes of literary studies illustrate the general thesis with regard to specific examples. Such gestures are alien to Blanchot, whose essays are closer in form to the meditation than to the demonstration. But it is this projection that guides the reflections, and sometimes very clearly. At the outset of the first of the Hölderlin essays, entitled 'Hölderlin and the Sacred Word', Blanchot writes:

> If one wishes to reflect on what is signified by the fact that the poem, that song exist, and if one claims to interrogate this fact from outside, this interrogation can only lead to Hölderlin, because here this question, experienced for itself and from within poetry, gave rise to the poem. (PF 118, 114)

The case of Hölderlin (studied here in Chapter 2) shows very well that if modern poetry is a 'poetry of poetry' (the phrase used by Heidegger with reference to Hölderlin), this designation cannot be equated with what is often understood by poetic or literary self-reflection (in some deconstructive analysis or in some avowedly post-modern works) – that is, a kind of meta-poetry, close in its meaning if not its method to literary theory or linguistics. To treat the question of poetry in Hölderlin in these terms could only be reductive, ignoring all that links it to the constitution of an entire poetic world, to an historical reflection, and to the elegiac and prophetic themes of the poems. Certainly, what is striking in any first reading of these poems is above all their religious dimension. In poems such as 'Bread and Wine', Hölderlin meditates on Greece and the world of Christ; this was the age in which the gods were living and present to man; in recollecting this historical moment, the poet is able to take the measure of the individualism and materialism of the world in which he finds himself, and to reflect on the possibility of poetry under modern conditions. The vocation of the poet, for Hölderlin, has to be conceived in relation to 'the sacred', 'the highest' (cf. as in his poem, 'The Poet's Vocation'). But this response only exacerbates the crisis in which poetry finds itself – since 'what use are the poets in the time of distress?', how can poetry exist, now that 'the father has turned his face away from men' ('Bread and Wine').

The passage we have cited points to what it is that is so distinctive about the structure and the mode of approach of this criticism. The study of Hölderlin, it suggests, is informed by an interrogation of the existence of the poem that is pursued 'from outside'. The tangential relationship of Blanchot's work to literary scholarship can be traced back to the imperatives of this interrogation. Blanchot's study is not confined to the exposition, in discursive form, of the thought expressed in Hölderlin's poems: it also repeats and, at times, elaborates the statement of the poems in the direction of its own response to the question of what it means 'that the poem exists'. The critical text is a *repetition* of the poetic text. This proximity is reflected in the reappearance of motifs from Hölderlin in Blanchot's own writing: a number of the essential themes of *L'Espace littéraire* – the condition of the poet as one of solitude and anticipation, the modern epoch as the time of distress, the poem as the event of a beginning – are prefigured in these essays on Hölderlin.

The same is true of the studies of Mallarmé (studied in Chapter 3). Mallarmé is granted a privileged status within Blanchot's historical perspective, not only because he devotes his career to a pure poetic realization, at the cost of a relatively limited output and many accusations of wilful obscurity, but also because the enterprise is accompanied by the poet's own commentary – first in the letters of the 1860s, which provide a dramatic and revealing narration of the process by which Mallarmé discovers his poetics, and then, in the later and more oblique prose texts, where he comments on contemporary poets and culture, and evokes the mysterious 'Work' which he may or may not be seriously engaged in writing, but which, even if it is only notional, gives the measure for the demands and the possibilities of poetry.

Many of these later prose texts reflect on the situation of literature in the historical conjuncture represented by late nineteenth-century Europe. The marginalization of poetry, to which Hölderlin gives mythic expression in dramatizing the fate of the poet in the time of the absence of gods, reappears in the more mundane context of contemporary French culture: 'for various reasons', the poet is 'excluded from all participation in the official deployments of beauty', and has to be content with performing the solitary rites of the poetic faith, and imagining the forms that a possible sovereignty of the poetic would take – recognizing, however, that nothing of the sort can be realized in the age in which he lives ('Richard Wagner, Revery of a French Poet').[4] But these texts are not primarily oriented around the

---

4   *Igitur, Divagations, Un Coup de dés.* Paris: Gallimard, 1976, 164. In English: *Divagations*. Trans. Barbara Johnson, Cambridge, MA: Harvard UP, 2007 (translation lightly modified for the present context).

despairing contrast of the poetic ideal with the contemporary urban reality, in the manner of the 'negative' Romanticism of the period of Baudelaire.[5] In Mallarmé, no less than in Hölderlin – though in a very different style – the marginalization of the poet that is imposed by from outside, the untenability of the ideals and privileges transmitted with the poetic tradition in a materialistic, technological and mediatized society, is absorbed into the poetic sphere and the question of the possibility of poetry becomes the productive tension out of which the poetry develops. The need for such a reflection, Mallarmé suggests, is at work already in the 'Crisis of Verse' – that is, the abandonment of the canonical verse forms, such as the alexandrine – that marks the poetic production of his period. In 'Music and Letters', Mallarmé writes:

> [I]n the upheavals, all to the credit of the recent generation, the act of writing scrutinized itself to its origin. Very far, at least, when it comes to the point, which I formulate thus: that is, whether there is a need for writing [. . .]
>
> Does something like Letters exist? Other than as the refinement (such was the convention in the classical ages) in the direction of their most polished form of expression of notions from all domains?[6]

For Blanchot these lines, from late in the poet's career, cast a retrospective light on the idea of the work sketched out in his early letters, indicating the radicality of the doubt to which it owed its inception. The 'Work' envisaged in these letters as the revelation of beauty and nothingness supposes that poetry is indeed something other than the artful expression of ideas originating in other domains. This work is to be created in accordance with an immanent necessity that is to be

---

5 On Romanticism and 'negative Romanticism', and Mallarmé's relation to these predecessors, see the introduction to Paul Bénichou's book of exegeses, *Selon Mallarmé*. Paris: Gallimard, 1995.

6 [D]ans des bouleversements, tout à l'acquit de la génération récente, l'acte d'écrire se scruta jusqu'en l'origine. Très avant, au moins, quant à un point, je le formule: – A savoir s'il y a lieu d'écrire [...] Quelque chose comme les Lettres existe-t-il; autre (une convention fut, aux époques classiques, cela) que l'affinement, vers leur expression burinée, des notions, en tout domaine. Igitur, Divagations, Un Coup de dés, 353. In English: *Divagations*, 185–186 (translation lightly modified for the present context).

attained through the elimination of chance. But it is also something more than an apotheosis of formal construction that is here imagined. Mallarmé's work – as he writes in his autobiographical letter to Verlaine – will be the Book itself, the one that every writer has worked upon, 'the Orphic explication of the earth'. A few lines after the text that we have cited above, in answer to the question that he has posed, Mallarmé writes: 'Yes, literature exists, and indeed, alone, in the exclusion of all else' (*Oui, que la littérature existe et, si l'on veut, seule, à l'exclusion de tout*).[7]

Each of the articles examined here returns to this project. The idea of poetic totality formulated by Mallarmé is seen as having its foundation in an initial decision that poetic language is essentially separate from language as we use it in the world, and that its effect cannot ultimately be understood in terms of representation, of reasoning and persuasion, or of the expression of feeling and interiority, even if it makes use of these elements. Mallarmé's 'Work' represents the rigorous elaboration of the consequences of this decision. Since the principle of this separation is also found in diverse forms in many other writers, and could even be seen as standing at the origin of the modern literary concept, one can begin to determine Blanchot's relation to literary criticism in this connection in a more general way than is possible through comparison of the exegeses of specific writers. The essential affirmation that sustains Blanchot's studies of Mallarmé is that this thinking of literature has the force of an historical event, and is not merely a reflection of shifts in culture, ideas or technology. For Blanchot, an understanding of the poetic here comes to light that had not been available to this point, and that alters its significance and its position in relation to our understanding of ourselves and the world. This does not mean that Mallarmé's work is granted a definitive authority: as with most of the writers he studies, Blanchot will distance certain elements that appear to him to be historical in the 'minor' sense, in that they bear the mark of their time. It does mean, however, that these studies are concerned, not so much with the accurate interpretation of Mallarmé's poetic system, considered as one among others, present to the synoptic gaze of literary history, but with elaborating the horizon in which these affirmations take on their full

---

7   Ibid. For the letter to Verlaine, *Igitur, Divagations, Un Coup de Dés,* 371-377; and the English *Divagations,* 1–7.

significance. This takes place not only through the sequence of critical essays about Mallarmé, but also through the poetics that is developed in the course of *La Part du feu* and *L'Espace littéraire*. Here again, as we observed with Hölderlin, there is close relationship between the interpretation of Mallarmé and Blanchot's own statement. Blanchot's presentation of the work, reading and writing can be seen as a repetition and an appropriation of central theses of Mallarmé's poetics: the silence that the work is capable of creating, the disappearance of the poet into his work, the ambiguity of the work between something that is made and its mere being.

For Blanchot, the key to understanding these figures lies in Mallarmé's understanding of language. This is not, however, a *theory* of language, or at least, not in the narrow sense of this term. Blanchot's work differs, not just in its style, but in its basic assumptions from the various kinds of literary theory in which the 'scientificity' of the theoretical claim is marked. Language is not considered here as an objective reality, divisible by analysis into set of sub-categories, but as the way that things are given to us in our occupation of the human world. Blanchot's inquiry is therefore engaged in the same essential area of thought as that which Heidegger approaches by way of the question of being. This comparison aids us by giving initial orientations for understanding the philosophical thought that develops alongside and in the course of Blanchot's literary criticism (and to which we turn in Chapter 4). The reference to death and absence which is striking for any first acquaintance with Blanchot's texts does not, I suggest, signify any kind of pessimistic or nihilistic world view, any kind of ultimately negative assessment of human prospects. Like the thought of being in Heidegger, it provides the terms for thinking what is presupposed in inhabiting the human world, and in relating to things in the mode of language. For Blanchot, the fact that we encounter things in their meanings, that we understand them in relation to our own possibilities, supposes that we have an anticipatory relation to death. It lies in the consequence of this understanding that language is not solely a means of knowing and manipulating things in the world, an exercise of human power and freedom. For the relation to death is not itself characterized by the distance and freedom that it gives us in relation to things in the world, when we are speaking and writing. It is to the ambiguities of this relation, Blanchot proposes, that we must turn in order to interpret the possibility that has come to be designated as literature. To make this affirmation requires, however, (as we see in Chapter 5) a critical re-examination of the categories through which literature is familiar to us, since these categories tend rather to conceal its true sense: for this reason, the questioning of these categories in modern literature solicits a philosophical thought for its explication.

The work of Heidegger has an important place in this study, since it aids in recognizing premises that are indicated rather elliptically in Blanchot. The elucidatory role given to Heideggerean thought inevitably comes at the expense of other figures (Bataille, Levinas, Sartre, Paulhan and others) who also have a strong presence as interlocutors and conceptual resources in Blanchot's texts. However, the comparison is not undertaken with an interest to documenting the historical context – an immense task in the case of Blanchot, of which this study can only anticipate certain strategically chosen moments. Heidegger's text serves here to understand the consistently maintained distance from disciplinary forms and practices of knowledge that is accomplished by the language of Blanchot's text. The question posed by a literary criticism such as Blanchot's is close, to that raised by Paul Ricoeur when he writes that:

> With Heidegger's philosophy, we are always engaged in going back to the foundations, but we are left incapable of beginning the movement of return which would lead from the fundamental ontology to the properly epistemological questions of the status of the human sciences. And yet a philosophy which breaks the dialogue with the sciences is no longer addressed to anything but itself.[8]

Ricoeur's comments lay the fault, if it is one, on Heidegger himself, rather than on the sciences, although from Heidegger's point of view, it could certainly also be put the other way around, since his thought claims to open up something which is *a priori* excluded by the forestructure of scientific knowledge procedures, an address which they will not 'hear' (the call of being). This divergence between knowledge

---

8 *Hermeneutics and the Human Sciences: Essays on Language, Action and Interpretation.* Ed. and trans. John. H. Thompson. NY: Cambridge UP, 1981, 59; see also 88–89.

and 'thinking' (the term he comes to adopt in place of 'philosophy' for his own enterprise) is essential to Heidegger's work which, in going back to the foundations, separates truth and knowledge and limits the monopoly of the scientific conception of truth. And yet the question of the practical disconnection between the two modes, identified by Ricoeur, is not greatly elaborated, and remains a vexed issue, as one sees in an external way in the difficulties of integrating Heideggerean thought into an ongoing project of research and teaching. These remarks are intended more to point to a problem than to make any definitive statement on the reception of Heidegger, which is extensive and diverse. In the case of Blanchot, however, the dilemma can be stated with less qualification, since his work really has been very little assimilated into the field of literary studies, despite the fact that it makes up a substantial body of work in the field, and one that is agreed in principle by nearly all to be of high quality – of high 'literary' quality, at least, if not a work recommended for imitation.

The proximity and the distance of critical commentary and philosophical thought in Blanchot will form the horizon of the studies that follow. In Blanchot's interpretation, as we will see, the intense revaluation and critique to which modern writers subject the concept of literature is deeply bound up with the critique of modern epistemology and the questioning of its foundations initiated by Heidegger. This is a point, then, at which the separate enterprises of thinking and knowledge (in the Heideggerean sense of this division) come into contact by virtue of the phenomenon itself. Ordinarily, Heidegger claims (in 'Was heisst Denken'), the sciences 'do not think' – a needlessly provocatively formulation, perhaps, if it only means that the question of being is not necessary for the accomplishment of scientific research, something with which the majority of those engaged presently in thinking the theory of literary studies or 'the epistemology of the human sciences' (to use Ricoeur's term) would be only too happy to agree. But if it turns out that the question of being, and the divergence of truth and knowledge that it requires, is necessary for the understanding of phenomena within a specific regional object field – such as that of modern literature – then here at least, this peaceful coexistence through mutual avoidance may no longer be viable.

1 The Modern Age and the 'Work' of Literature

The essays collected in Blanchot's works of literary criticism must surely count as one of the most significant studies of literature in the Romantic and post-Romantic period. Few other works offer a comparative study of modern literature of such extent, able to bring together Hölderlin, Baudelaire, Mallarmé, Rilke, Kafka, Proust, Valéry, Mann, Musil, Artaud and many others. The emphasis on poetry and on works from the twentieth century, in particular, is exceptional – there is perhaps no other major work of comparative literature in which these textual areas provide the main frame of reference. This concentration reflects something more than an empirical area of specialization: the studies are guided and informed by a theoretical and historical reflection on what is distinctive about the situation and the characteristics of *modern* literature. Although it is not always emphasized, the historical theme is subtly present in many of the studies of individual writers, and it can serve as a means of approach to the properly critical dimension of Blanchot's writings on literature.

The primary concern with modern writers is marked at all periods in Blanchot's work, but it is only with a group of texts written in close proximity, in the period immediately after the publication of *La Part du feu* in 1949, that the historical dimension is directly addressed. In 'The Museum, Art and Time', a long essay in response to Malraux's *Les Voix du silence*, first published in 1950–1951 (and collected in the later volume, *L'Amitié*), Blanchot reflects on the emancipation of modern art from religious and political imperatives and its devotion to purely plastic and formal values, and considers the link between this moment in the history of art and the emergence of the museum. Similar themes, developed now with reference to literature as well as art – above all with reference to modern poetry – reappear in 'Literature and the Original Experience', first published as an article in two parts in *Les Temps modernes* in 1952, and then placed as the conclusion of *L'Espace littéraire* (1955) Comparison of the two versions shows that the essay has been extensively revised for its republication in the context of the book (the revisions between the journal and the book publication of Blanchot's essays are often quite significant, and can sometimes lend valuable assistance in interpreting difficult texts). Moreover, much of its argument is restated in an essay entitled 'Where Is Literature Going?', published in two parts the following year, during the period in which most of the essays that now make up *L'Espace littéraire* were being composed. The first part of this text, again somewhat revised, appeared as 'The Disappearance of Literature' in *Le Livre à venir* (1959). The second part of the essay was never collected in book form by Blanchot, although parts of it were re-distributed into several texts of *L'Espace littéraire*, including 'Literature and the Original Experience' in its final form.[1]

The restatements, revisions and re-distributions of text that all these pieces go through in their definitive appearance reflect the working out of a historical dimension that was not present or at least not very marked in Blanchot's work up to this point. Modern art and literature now appears as traversed and gathered together by a consistent intentional movement, visible through a multiplicity of its forms. This understanding becomes possible through an interpretation of the modern epoch more generally. In its language and its structures, this interpretation often recalls (explicitly or implicitly) the thought of Hegel. In the preface to the *Phenomenology of Spirit*, Hegel writes:

> It is further not hard to see that our time is a time of birth and transition into a new era. Spirit has broken away from its former world of existence and imaging [*vorstellen*]; it is about to sink all that into the past, and is busy shaping itself anew.[2]

To a remarkable extent, Blanchot not only assumes Hegel's affirmation that modernity represents a new and original historical situation, but also takes over much of his interpretation of the basic character

---

[1] It is now available in *La Condition critique: articles 1945–1998*. Ed. Christophe Bident. Paris: Gallimard (Cahiers de la NRF), 2010, 191–204.
[2] *Hegel's Preface to the Phenomenology of Spirit*. Translation and commentary by Yirmiyahu Yovel. Princeton, NJ: Princeton University Press, 2005, 82.

of 'our time'.³ Hegel's thought, it is true, is mediated here by French commentators such as Kojève and Hyppolite whose interpretations, especially with regard to religion and politics, are closer to the left Hegelians and to Marx than to the later Hegel of *The Philosophy of Right*. But in this modified form, Hegelian thought serves to conceptualize the essential decisions that make the modern period what it is. In two of the texts, Blanchot refers to Hegel's often discussed thesis that art is a 'thing of the past'. It is worth citing both versions, since the slight variations help in understanding Blanchot's construction of the modern (which is our only concern here). In 'The Future and the Question of Art' (EL VII.i), Blanchot, glossing Hegel's thesis, writes:

> from the moment that the absolute has consciously become identified with the work of history, art has no longer been able to satisfy the need for an absolute (*à partir du jour où l'absolu est devenu consciemment travail de l'histoire, l'art n'est plus capable de satisfaire le besoin d'absolu*). Relegated to our interiority, it has lost its reality and its necessity; all that it had that was genuinely true and living now belongs to the world, and to real work in the world. (EL 284, 214)

And in 'The Disappearance of Literature':

> Art is no longer capable of providing access to the absolute. (*l'art n'est plus capable de porter le besoin d'absolu*). What counts absolutely is henceforth the accomplishment of the world, the seriousness of action, and the task of real freedom. (LV 265, 195)

Hegel's judgement on the fate of art is the expression of an historical evidence, of a new sense of 'what counts absolutely'. The absolute, the

---

3 The identification of the philosophical question of modernity with Hegel has become relatively common in the wake of Kojève's lectures and the reawakening of interest in Hegel in France. Its validity is also defended in the first two chapters of Jürgen Habermas's *The Philosophical Discourse of Modernity*. Trans. Frederick G. Lawrence. MIT Press, 1987. Habermas writes: 'Hegel was the first philosopher to develop a clear concept of modernity. We have to go back to him, if we want to understand the internal relation between modernity and rationality, which had been self-evident until Max Weber, and which today has been placed in question' (4).

unconditioned point from which the understanding of the self and the world proceeds, has shifted position. In the past, it was located in a transcendent principle such as God or the metaphysical principles of the cosmos; now it is identified with free human reason in its real and historically determined situation. The modern epoch is that in which the human takes possession of itself and responsibility for itself, recognizing its own rationality as the immanent truth of all reality. In his account of this process, Hegel emphasizes that human reason, unlike preceding absolute instances (the divine, the sovereign), is not given as absolute by its nature or essence. As it comes to know itself, it discovers also that it is conditioned and limited by natural, physical realities, by the diversity and the constraints of existing laws and institutions, by the contradictions it finds both within itself and between its representatives. Humanity – or free rationality (Spirit, *Geist* in Hegel) – is only *in principle* an absolute: its vocation is to make itself in reality into what it is already by its principle.

The mode of being whose emergence is described by Hegel is active, engaged in a process of becoming, transforming (or 'negating') itself in order to realize itself. In the *Philosophy of History*, Hegel writes: 'Spirit (*Geist*) essentially acts: it makes itself into what it is at first only potentially (*an sich*), into its deed, its work; in this way it becomes an object for itself, and is present to itself'.[4] One finds the same trait underlined in Blanchot: present-day man is 'given over ... to the decision to realize himself, to become free of nature and of being through work and through effective action' (EL 311, 233). The threshold of modernity is attained at the moment that this decision has been assumed. The world has now to become the human world, a world submitted to the dictates of the free and rational human will. Henceforth, 'what counts absolutely is the accomplishment of the world, the seriousness of action and the task of real freedom' (LV 265, 195 cited above).

In 'The Future and the Question of Art' (EL VII.i), this understanding of the modern ethos provides the horizon for a critical assessment of modern aesthetics. The section is useful for a consideration of Blanchot's work as criticism, since it indicates how his work

---

4 *Vorlesungen über die Philosophie der Weltgeschichte. Werkausgabe*, Bd.12. Frankfurt a.M.: Suhrkamp, 1986, 99. (My translation). The passage is to be found in *Introduction to the Philosophy of History*. Trans. Leo Rauch. Indianapolis: Hackett, 1988, 77.

would situate itself in relation to the conflicts that shape the critical field. The discussion begins with the alternative between those for whom the literary or artistic work is 'an object of contemplation rather than usage, sufficient in itself, resting in itself', and those for whom it only has its meaning when considered within the wider context of human action and history.[5] The conflict is well known in literary criticism, where critical positions have often defined themselves in relation to the polarity between a view of the work as a self-contained aesthetic form, on the one hand, and a view of the work as a particular mode of historical and cultural discourse, on the other. For Blanchot, this debate takes for granted the terms of the modern self-understanding.

> Both [positions] recognize in man the excellence of a power and in the artist the exercise of a form of this power, demanding work, discipline, study. (280, 211–212)

To the extent that interaction with art is primarily the production and the evaluation of 'works', it has its measure in accomplishment, it is suggested. The claim for the aesthetic is thus ultimately a claim for a distinct sphere of work, albeit one with its own conditions and procedures. Whatever distinctions and privileges this sphere may be allowed, it remains subject to the evidence and the criteria of work.[6] Even if it moves according to its 'own little laws', the artistic domain – inasmuch as it is a kind of work – falls within and will contribute to 'the total human work and the affirmation of the universal light' (281, 213).

---

5 For an illuminating philosophical discussion of this division, close to the issues in this text, see Jacques Taminiaux, 'The Death of Art and the Aesthetic Attitude' in *Poetry, Speculation and Judgment*. Trans. Michael Gendre. Albany: SUNY Press, 1993, 55–72. Taminiaux's analysis indicates that the terms of this debate correspond to the division between the Kantian and the Hegelian directions in aesthetics. See also Peter V. Zima, *The Philosophy of Modern Literary Theory*. London: Athlone, 1999, especially the introductory chapter, which (independently) analyses the history of literary theory in terms of a Kantian and a Hegelian stream.
6 The link between the new philosophical importance accorded to 'work' in Hegelian thought and the culture and ideology of nineteenth- and twentieth-century Europe, is studied in the excellent chapter on 'The Problem of Work' in Karl Löwith, *From Hegel to Nietzsche: The Revolution in Nineteenth-Century Thought*. Trans. David E. Green. London: Constable, 1964, 263–288.

6   Blanchot and Literary Criticism

Once art and literature are produced within a horizon that is commanded by the criteria of work and historical action, however, artists and writers are compelled to recognize that their work is a relatively marginal and not very effective form of activity:

> In the past, art was able to reconcile itself with other absolute demands: painting served the gods, poetry made them speak: but these powers were not of this world, and since their reign was outside of time, they did not measure the services that were performed for them in terms of their efficacity in real time. Art has also been in the service of politics, but politics then was not wholly in the service of action, and action had not become conscious of itself as the universal demand (*l'exigence universelle*). (283, 213)

In Blanchot's writings, there is a consistent, if not always explicit sense that what is here called 'the universal demand' is one that is difficult to accept, as well as the decision that it *should* be accepted. This is present in the text we have been examining in the implication that the claim for aesthetic autonomy (the work with 'its own little laws') lacks something in transparency and even sincerity – that it seeks to gain recognition by the criteria of work and action, while at the same time withdrawing from their full implications.[7] In contrast with the various accommodations through which nineteenth-century culture in fact maintains a very elevated conception of the value of art, Hegel's thesis of the 'end of art' is credited for the stringency with which it draws the consequences for art of a free historical mode of existence

The same ethical–political tendency appears in the next section of the essay, dealing with the Romantic affirmation that links art to the inner sovereignty of the self, and thus frees it from the demand of effective realization.[8] The treatment of this phenomenon is phased in two separate developments. In the first of these, it is suggested

---

7   The subordination of aesthetic claims to the 'universal demand' of work and effectiveness does not lend weight to the view of Jameson that Blanchot is a proponent of an 'ideology of aesthetic autonomy', Frederic Jameson, *A Singular Modernity: Essay on the Ontology of the Present*. NY: Verso, 2002, 183.

8   Blanchot's response to Romanticism is more complex than these rather schematic remarks indicate; see also 'Atheism, Humanism and the Cry', and the text on German Romanticism, entitled 'The Atheneum', both in *L'Entretien infini*.

that, contrary to appearances, the revolt in the name of subjective passion against the criteria of work and effectivity does not express a fundamentally different motivation from the modern assertion of historical freedom, but that it constitutes rather an integral moment within its emergence. At the same time that modern humanity makes the external world into a field of objectivity, present for the subject and under its power, it also tends to intensify the uniqueness and the irreducibility of the subject as self. The two moments support and promote each other. The more the self gains in depth and autonomy, the more it reinforces the realizing will that has its foundation within the subject; likewise, the greater the mastery over the world, the greater the possibility for the human subject to develop its consciousness of its own inner freedom (cf. 287–288, 217). In a second development, Blanchot proceeds to assign this dialectic to a specific historical situation, that which Blanchot refers to as 'humanism'. This claim depends upon a schema of the different historical meanings assigned to art, which Blanchot, acknowledging its 'Hegelian' style, terms 'the dialectic of the work' (EL 305, 229).[9] Art and poetry, it is here suggested, first acquires their meaning from the function they serve in cult and religion: in its most original form, with the hymn and the temple, art makes present the divinity; later, in a slightly more secular age, it represents the gods, and gives them form (the reference is no doubt to Greek art). In the 'humanist' moment, which for Blanchot embraces the period between the Renaissance and Romanticism, the artistic possibility becomes one of the means by which the human subject discovers itself and claims its rights against the divine order announced in myth and religion. Art does not only then represent the human individual in its subject matter: the artistic activity understands (and sometimes represents)

---

9 The resemblance is more one of general style than of detail. Blanchot's scheme diverges significantly from the historical scheme given in Hegel's *Aesthetics*, and seems to owe more to Hölderlin whose thought is also very present in these texts at certain points, and in whom there is a stronger sense of a sharp division, an epochal break, between the ancient world, where the divine is present and active, and modernity as the historical period that is conditioned by the absence of the gods. It should be noted that the philosophical–historical reflection, which begins with these texts on modernity and literature, is pursued in many texts in *L'Amitié* and *L'Entretien infini*, and attains a complexity that cannot be represented here. This is an aspect of Blanchot's thought that has been relatively little discussed in the reception of his work.

itself as the expression of human freedom and mastery. It is at this moment, then, that the artistic possibility is particularly identified with concepts and figures that underline the elevated power of the artist – the idea of genius, the figure of the artist as the great individual, the understanding of art as the medium of the subjective vision. The historical scheme serves to limit the validity of this set of concepts by assigning their legitimacy to a particular historical phase. For in the more recent modern period – in the 'new era' that Hegel announces – human rationality and autonomy no longer need to be discovered, but only to be accomplished; henceforth it is rather 'in the development of technical forms of conquest that it finds the dialectical vitality which assure it of its goal' (EL 288, 217). When art continues to be given its meaning by the reverence for the artist as the exceptional individual, what is actually taking place, Blanchot suggests, is a reaction against the demands of modernity. Art becomes the preserve of the individual subjectivity, and as such, it represents a point of resistance to the demands of modern science, politics and dialectical reason, which are essentially collective and impersonal. The notion of 'creativity' takes on its full meaning in relation to this historical tension; if this term has found such resonance, to the point that it is still co-terminous with the artistic sphere in the popular imagination, it is because it is able to effect a delicate conceptual negotiation between two antagonistic demands. On the one hand, the appeal of creativity reflects the value of power and realization. But at the same time, this creation does not fall under the jurisdiction of rational purpose and method; it remains bound to the spontaneity of the artist, thus 'protecting him against the anonymity of collective work, reassuring him that he remains the individual, a man in the great style (*l'homme de grand format*)' (EL 290, 219). From this point of view, one can understand the mythical allure that the figure of the artist and the poet assumes in the modern period.

In the course of 'The Future and the Question of Art', the chapter whose movement we have been following here, Blanchot formulates the ethos of the modern age in terms of the priority of work and objective accomplishment. From this standpoint, the claims that have perpetuated a sense of the importance of art during this age – the autonomy of the artistic sphere, the immortality of the artistic creation, the originality of artistic genius – appear as a reaction against the implications of this ethos. In Blanchot's critique, moreover, the reaction is seen as mobilized, not so much against what it means for the artists, considered as a kind of social or professional group, as against what it means for individuality, the value that artistic creativity is enlisted to preserve. At the end of the chapter, the point of view shifts a little, as Blanchot turns to consider another movement in modern art and literature:

> However, by another and no less remarkable movement, art, as the presence of man to himself, cannot be contented with the humanist transformation that history reserves for it. Art has now to become its own presence. What it wants to affirm is art. What it seeks, what it tries to accomplish, is the essence of art. (EL 291, 219)

To this point, Blanchot's reflection in this essay has been concerned with the aesthetic *concepts* by which art and literature are valued and defined; now, however, it is evidently a question of certain works. The use of 'art' as an impersonal subject – a frequent and rather disconcerting gesture in Blanchot – indicates a common intention, shared by multiple artists and works. The shift in modern painting away from the representational mode is said to exemplify a wider movement which 'draws all the arts towards themselves, concentrates them in the concern for their own essence, makes them present and essential' (292, 220).[10] In this passage, Mallarmé, Cézanne and Schoenberg are named: a similar passage mentions Kafka, Hölderlin, and Rilke, among others (286, 216). The fact that these lists include all the writers studied in *L'Espace littéraire* suggests that this is a book *about* this historical formation, and that the essays on individual writers can be inscribed within the more general problem of interpretation posed by this phenomenon. This historical projection is something new in Blanchot's work. In the preceding collection, *La Part du feu*, a more diverse and 'essayistic' work, a degree closer to the origins of Blanchot's criticism in the literary reviews, the connections drawn between the essays are made at the level of the theory of language and literature. The historical dimension here sketched out addresses

---

10 At this point Blanchot also refers to the writings on Malraux: here we see the link between this essay and 'The Museum, Art and Time' (collected in *L'Amitié*), Blanchot's first sustained treatment of art and modernity.

precisely what remains unexplained in *La Part du feu*, and in earlier texts – namely, why it is specifically in relation to writers from nineteenth- and twentieth-century Europe that Blanchot develops the philosophical questions of language and literature by which his texts are preoccupied.

The interpretation of modernity provides the horizon within which this phenomenon is seen.[11] The movement to accomplish 'the essence of art', Blanchot observes, belongs to the same historical moment during which 'the absolute takes the form of history, when the concerns and interests of the times are no longer compatible with the sovereignty of art' (292, 220). 'Modern literature' and 'modern art' – terms Blanchot uses from time to time, certainly not as period categories, in the narrow sense, but also without too much reserve – are to be understood, then, not primarily in the context of political, technological or social changes, but in relation to modernity, as a more general transformation at the level of our self-understanding and our relation to the world.[12]

The text that we have been reading ends in posing the question as to how this convergence should be interpreted. The next two sections of 'Literature and the original experience' (EL VII.ii and iii) then take a somewhat different direction. It would certainly be possible to consider the exposition of the work of art and the act of writing in these sections – and indeed, in *L'Espace littéraire* as a whole – as the indirect paths of a response to the historical question. But if we are to better understand the terms of the question – above all the claim, very schematically indicated to this point, that the modern work wants to 'accomplish the essence of art' (291, 219) – more is to be gained by turning to the essay entitled 'The Disappearance of Literature' (LV IV.i). It is characteristic of the circling movement of Blanchot's reflection that

---

11 This interpretation develops throughout the course of *L'Espace littéraire* and subsequent works. It will be studied here in greater detail in our Chapter 4.
12 This horizon is not often explicitly present in the essays on particular writers, although there are often historical indications that could allow one to develop the connection. The essay on Kafka in *L'Espace littéraire* refers to the decline of the religious foundation in the Jewish community to which Kafka belonged (67–76, 59–62); the essay on Rilke situates his reflection on death in relation to 19th century individualism (153–157, 121–124); likewise, the essays on Musil and Broch in *Le Livre à venir* place their thought in relation to the scientific and logical imperatives of early twentieth century thought. Other examples could be added.

a question suspended in one text will be resumed (typically without being signalled as such) in a later text.

'The Disappearance of Literature' begins at precisely the point that the text that we have been reading comes to an end. It is striking, Blanchot here remarks, that at the very moment at which art seems to have been definitively assigned to a marginal place in the interest of 'the accomplishment of the world, the seriousness of action, the task of real freedom', one sees works of art develop a deeper and more demanding sense of their own being *as* art (LV 266, 196). The implication, evidently, is that modern literature can be understood as a response to a modification in the social meaning assigned to art, in function of a more general shift in priorities. But if the vision of the world as a possibility and a task for a free historical subjectivity constitutes the *conditions* under which modern art and literature originate, this does not mean that it simply *explains* these transformations. The emergence of a technical, industrialized, and mediatized society promotes and even compels a revaluation of the transmitted privileges of art: the overcoming of art contained in the modern idea of the subject receives immediate expression in many characteristic modern phenomena, in utilitarian ideology, in bureaucratic and commercial society, in the rise of popular culture, to name only a few (cf. LV 268, 196). And yet, Blanchot claims, this critical pressure coincides with an 'experience that art and literature traverse in their own name, and which exposes them to a radical contestation' (*cette critique étrangère répond à l'expérience que la littérature et l'art conduisent au nom d'eux-mêmes et qui les expose à une contestation radicale*):

> In this contestation, the skeptical genius of Valéry and the firmness of his position cooperates with the violent affirmations of the surrealists. It may seem that there is nothing in common between Valéry, Hoffmanstahl and Rilke. And yet Valéry writes: 'My verses have had no other interest for me than to suggest reflections on the poet', and Hoffmanstahl that: 'The innermost essence of the poet is nothing other than that he is aware of being a poet'. As for Rilke, it would not be misleading to say that his poetry is the theory, in song, of the poetic act. In each of these three cases, the poem is opened on to the experience which makes it possible; it is the strange movement that

goes from the work to the origin of the work. The work has itself become the infinite and anxious search for its own source. (LV 269, 196–197)

The historical scope of the claim is reiterated a little later, when Blanchot claims that the same analysis would be valid for Hölderlin, a century earlier, as for René Char, a generation later than the poets cited. Such affinities, Blanchot claims, point to a form of continuity (*une durée*) that is 'very different than that apprehended by simple historical analysis' (269, 198). What is referred to here as 'simple historical analysis', we may suppose, is the kind of historical categories that ordinarily organize and guide literary studies: categories of period and nation, schools and movements, styles and world-views. Given the determining role of such categories in literary studies, their absence in Blanchot can be assumed to be one of the factors that has worked to slow his reception within the field.[13] This absence, however, does not mean that his work proceeds on ahistorical principles, but that it is concerned with a kind of historicity that only becomes visible if one sees the works within a horizon that extends beyond their immediate cultural and historical context.

The point of the comparison between Valéry, Hofmannstahl and Rilke is not to identify self-reflexivity as the dominant note of modern art and literature. It is true that modern poetry and art is often accompanied by and informed by a discourse carried on in letters, essays, manifestos, intent on elaborating or supplementing the sense of the work itself, and this may well be a feature that crosses narrower period distinctions. In the passage we have cited, however, literary reflexivity is presented as a sign of a more fundamental transformation: 'the strange movement that goes from the work to the origin of the work' (ibid). The artistic activity, then, is no longer given its meaning and its direction primarily by *the work*, in the sense of the completed artefact. The priority of the creation of the work, which seems so self-evident, has its historical presuppositions. It can only prevail when artistic and literary work rests

---

13 The effect on literary studies of the 'field coverage principle of organization' is analysed by Gerald Graff in *Professing Literature: An institutional history*. Chicago: University of Chicago Press, 1987.

in and is carried by an understanding of what the literary is, what art is – in other words, by an operative conception of 'the essence of art'. Such an understanding need not be theoretically explicit and developed; no doubt it is all the more effective, all the more 'productive', when it is tacit or naïve; then the artist and the writer can devote themselves to the excellence of the work itself, unburdened by any kind of reflective consciousness. When it becomes apparent that this 'essence' is not given, however, then literary and artistic activity is compelled into the circular movement by which it becomes the search for its own origin: the work becomes the path that allows 'the approach to that which makes the work possible: art, literature, and that which is dissimulated behind these words' (271, 199).

Blanchot interprets the entire work of certain writers as animated by such a search: this is the case, as we will see, in the studies of Hölderlin and Mallarmé. But this projection is also present in a more extensive way as a set of traits that mark the relation of the modern artist or writer to his work, to his public, and to the prevailing concepts and institutions of art and literature. One such trait, Blanchot here suggests, is the shift in the model of the artistic career from the serial production of works to the movement of a search. The artistic career is now 'a passion' which sees 'in each work only an inconclusive step along the path of a search which we too recognize in the unfinished canvases, the pictures which seem open; the path is now the only essential work' (EL 315, 235). The reference here is to painting, but one can think also, in the literary context, of the role of the diary and the journal, to which Blanchot is often attentive (for example, in 'Kafka and the Demand of the Work' EL III.ii, 'Joubert and Space', 'The Diary and the Story' LV II.iv, III.viii). The sketch or the fragment takes priority over the completed work inasmuch as it is able to 'lead [the artist] to a certain point', even if it has to be abandoned, in order to 'go beyond that point' (LV 271, 199).

It is a similar impulse, Blanchot goes on to suggest, that is at work in the destructive and transgressive tendencies of literary modernism – in the abandonment of literary conventions, such as verse-form or the pattern of the well-made plot, in the critique of the elevated sentiments and the spiritual ideals from which art had drawn its cultural authority and prestige, and perhaps most tellingly, in the dissolution or revision of generic norms.[14] Such phenomena are often analysed in cultural terms; they can be seen, for example, as reflecting the decline of a set of shared values, the increased prestige of individualism and originality, or the entry of techniques of publicity into the sphere of art. But it is also possible to see these kinds of consideration as secondary, and to locate the origin of such transformations in a crisis in the very idea of literature and art (cf. LV 278, 204). It is significant, Blanchot remarks, that as genres, forms, ideals are abandoned, the word 'literature', once a name for the excesses of writing, comes to acquire renewed power and attraction:

> All that matters is the book, such as it is, far from genres, outside the categories, prose, poetry, novel, documentary, under which it refuses to be ordered, which it denies the power to fix its place and determine its form. A book no longer belongs to a genre, every book belongs solely to literature, as if this term contained in advance, in their generality, the secrets and formulae which alone would permit to give to what is written the reality of a book. It is very much as if, the genres having dissipated, literature now affirms itself alone in the mysterious clarity that it emanates, and that each literary creation revives in multiplying it – as if, then, there was an essence of literature. (272–273, 200–201)

With this last conditional, Blanchot seems to withdraw the understanding that had been developed up until this point. There follows a series of paradoxical formulations which would seem to render the search for the essence of art (or literature) untenable. Thus, Blanchot writes that 'the essence of literature is precisely to elude any determination of its essence, any affirmation that would stabilize or even realize it' (273, 201). If literature is the preoccupation of modern writers, it is as something that 'one only approaches in turning away from it, that

---

14 This identification of the antagonism between genre and modern literature is one of the relatively few areas in which Blanchot's work is cited within the wider field of literary criticism: cf. Tzvetan Todorov, *Genres in Discourse*. Trans. Catherine Porter. Cambridge UP, 1990, 13–15. John Frow, *Genre*. Routledge, 2005, 26–28. On the dissolution of genre in modern literature, see the collection of essays: *L'Éclatement des genres au vingtième siècle*. Ed. Marc Dambre and Monique Gosselin-Noat. Paris: Presse de la Sorbonne Nouvelle, 2001.

one only grasps where one goes beyond (…)': literature only comes to itself, to what it is essentially, in going outside of itself, in becoming other than itself: each writer has to respond alone to the question that is posed by the existence of literature (272–274, 200–201).

These remarks should be seen as a clarification and a qualification of the first, more schematic indications of the intention of the modern work rather than as a revision of the conception. The problem here is that any interpretation of this phenomenon necessarily implies a decision on what is in question – namely, 'the essence of art' – and by this decision enters into the history it seeks to comprehend. The complexities of the formulations here are surely meant to mark a distance with the 'symbolist' version of this history, for which the task of the modern poet tends to be framed as the realization of an essence, often understood in idealist or neo-Platonic terms.[15] But it is not merely a question of a precaution with regard to 'essentialism', by now a rather docile polemical opponent in any case.[16] One of the consequences of Blanchot's historical perspective would be to locate the symbolist current, which envisages art and poetry as a perhaps never attainable ideal, within the same overarching historical development as the avant-gardists who strip these terms of all meaning and value. For all that separates them, these two essential currents of literary modernity each have their point of departure in the recognition that literature cannot be taken for granted, that it remains to be discovered. What is sought, however, Blanchot specifies, is not literature as 'a definite and sure reality, as an ensemble of forms, or even as a determinate mode of activity' (272, 200). This qualification signals

---

15   The characterization of the ambition of modern art and literature in terms of a will to 'accomplish the essence of art' seems at first glance to invoke the 'pure poetry' of Paul Valéry, a conception which was not intended as an innovation, but only to formalize a tendency which he recognized in predecessors such as Poe, Baudelaire and Mallarmé. See on this question, Valéry's 1920 essay, 'Avant Propos à la connaissance d'une déesse'. *Oeuvres*. Tome I. Paris: Gallimard, 1957, 1269–1280.

16   Consideration of the use of the language of 'essence', frequent in Blanchot's texts would require discussion of the sense that 'essence' has in Heidegger (e.g. *das Wesen der Wahrheit, das Wesen der Kunst*). When Blanchot speaks in these texts of 'the essence of art', the sense is close to a relatively straightforward usage defined by Heidegger, when he writes that 'in this connection, "essence" is understood as the inner ground of possibility of what is initially and generally admitted as known'. *Pathmarks*. Trans. William McNeil. Cambridge: Cambridge UP, 1998, 143.

that the literary contestation of the norms of art cannot be inscribed into the tempting historical narrative, for which they would appear as the first forms of a fully demystified 'theoretical' understanding, reducing any kind of idealist or theological prestige, and identifying the literary with specific operations, mechanisms or structures of language.[17]

In order to see the positive sense of Blanchot's paradoxes, it helps to be attentive to their continuity with an ongoing thread of his reflection. In 'Literature and the Right to Death', for example, in a passage that anticipates the historical discussion here at issue, it is stated (though not, it must be said, explained) that, while one can define the novel or the poem, literature is the '*élément de vide*' that refuses definition, the 'caustic force' that dissolves the reflection that would seek to define it (PF 295, 302). And in a footnote in *L'Espace littéraire*, Blanchot writes that the generic indetermination of modern literature manifests the 'work' of literature 'to affirm itself in its essence in destroying distinctions and limits' (*ce travail profond de la littérature qui cherche à s'affirmer dans son essence en ruinant les distinctions et les limites*, EL 292, 220).[18] The 'work' referred to at this point is *le travail*, signifying an action that is performed over time (and not *l'oeuvre*, the work that is created): that it is *un travail profond*, a 'deep' or 'subterranean' work, performed by 'literature', suggests surely that the effects of this negation do not coincide with the intention or meaning of any particular work. In other words, it attributes an *effective* unity to works and initiatives, beyond what they intend at the level of meaning or ideas. If literature 'affirms itself in its essence' in these works, it is not as something that is present, in the pure form, through the elimination of non-literary elements, as in Valéry's 'pure poetry', but as an unknown, a 'void-element' revealed only through the negation of the categories by which it is mediated and given the intelligibility of a particular kind of thing in the world – categories of genre, of value, even the unity of the writer or artist, as an identifiable voice and style (cf. EL 22, 28).

---

17 For Blanchot's critical reception of this tendency, see 'The search for the zero point' (LV IV.ii), and in particular the second part, dealing with Roland Barthes.
18 This conception is elaborated with regard to the novel in 'At the very extremity' (LV III.i): see also the first version of this text, 'D'un art sans avenir' in *La Condition Critique: Articles 1945–1998*, 228–237.

The Modern Age and the 'Work' of Literature 17

This is precisely the sense that is given to modern literature in the prefatory 'Note' with which Blanchot gives an initial orientation to his next work, the immense meditation that is *L'Entretien infini*:

> Certainly, in all countries and all languages, books continue to appear, some of which are considered works of criticism or reflection, while others are referred to as novels or as poems. It is likely that such designations will continue to be used, just as there will still be books, long after the concept of the book has become obsolete. Nonetheless, it is necessary to make this remark: since Mallarmé (to reduce him to a name and this name to a point of reference), what has tended to make sterile such distinctions is that through them, and more important than them, there has come to light the experience of something that we continue to call "literature" but with a renewed seriousness, and, moreover, with quotation marks. Essays, novels, poems seem only to exist, only to be written, in order to allow the work (*le travail*) of literature (considered now as a singular power or a position of sovereignty) to accomplish itself, and through this work, to open up the question: 'what does it mean that something like art or literature should exist?' (*Qu'est-ce qui est en jeu par ce fait que quelque chose comme l'art or la littérature existerait?*) This is an extremely pressing question, and historically pressing (I refer here to certain texts of *L'Espace littéraire* and to *Le Livre à venir*, as well as to the pages entitled "La Littérature et le droit à la mort"), but one that a secular tradition of aestheticism has obscured and continues to obscure. (EI vi, xi)

Blanchot is sparing with such self-reflective gestures, and this prefatory note assumes all the more importance for the indication it provides on the continuity between the literary critical studies of the 1940s and 1950s and the more philosophical essays of *L'Entretien infini*. One sees that what is envisaged is still a collective and historical phenomenon, a plurality of initiatives with a deeper coherence than is apparent from their external differences. Mallarmé is named, not as the instigator of a definite movement or even as an influence, but as a point of reference, a figure in whose work one can begin to discern the direction of a transformation that passes through 'essays, poems, novels', without directly concerning these differentiations.

The phenomenon is visible externally in the erosion of distinctions of genre and the displacement of the completed work (here named 'the book') from its position as the *telos* of the literary process. But what is at issue here is not ultimately an intervention at the level of forms or conventions (cf. LV 284–285, 209), but a modification in the intention: the established divisions and priorities are subordinated in the interest of allowing 'the work of literature' (*le travail de la littérature*) to accomplish itself.

If we compare this presentation of the theme to those which we have examined in the earlier texts, one notes a significant difference in the *position* of the analysis. In *L'Espace littéraire* and *Le Livre à venir*, especially, Blanchot's criticism considers his subjects from a standpoint that is in unusually close proximity to the writers' own experience, reconstructing the path of their work and thought as if from within. This critical mode is reflected in the titles of certain of the essays: 'The Experience of Mallarmé', (EL II.ii), 'The Itinerary of Hölderlin' (EL Annex iv), 'The Experience of Proust' (LV I.ii). In the more general, literary-historical essays in these volumes that we have been studying here, this perspective is present in the concern with the writer's experience of the insufficiency of his art before the criteria of work and realization, and in the representation of the passion and the search for art that results. *L'Entretien infini*, on the other hand, assumes to a much greater extent the distance that is characteristic of philosophical and historical thought. From this standpoint, what is seen is the event of a transformation, even of a discovery: in the period here dated from the work of Mallarmé, a certain experience of "literature" has 'come to light': the term itself acquires a new sense (indicated by quotation marks) and occupies 'a position of sovereignty'; a little later, Blanchot re-describes this event as the emergence of 'writing', which 'through its own force has gradually liberated itself [...]' (EI vii, xii).

The effect of this affirmation of literature or writing is to pose the question of what it means 'that something like art or literature should exist'. The reference to this question recurs under different forms at each of the points at which the conclusions of this historical analysis begins to be drawn, and comes indeed to acquire something close to terminological or hermetic significance (cf. PF 293–295, 300–302; EL 321, 239): in 'The Atheneum', an essay in *L'Entretien infini* that revisits some of the topics studied here, Blanchot writes that with the writings of the early German Romantics, literature 'encounters its most dangerous sense – which is to declare itself in an interrogative mode' (EI 520, 354). Like the use of paradox noted earlier, this gesture may appear at first sight as a strategy of deferral. But this is not the case: on the contrary, this question indicates the inner coherence that Blanchot discerns in modern art and literature, the sense that it collaborates, more or less consciously, in a movement that has the character of a discovery, even of a revolution. One should note the assertion that this question is 'extremely pressing', provided that it is not defused by a 'secular tradition of aestheticism' – provided, that is, that these transformations are not reincorporated into literature in the sense that it has without quotation marks, as a collective noun for novels, plays and essays.

In order to see the significance of this 'work' of literature, one has to view it within the horizon from which it emerges. In the texts read here, this horizon is sketched out through the reference to Hegel: the interpretation of the modern epoch that is thus indicated is further developed in a series of evidently Hegelian themes in *L'Entretien infini* – the dialectic, the end of history, the completion of discourse, the book.[19] What is at stake in these developments is the articulation of a historical comprehension of who 'we' are, what philosophical decisions are supposed by our mode of relating to the world. It is only in relation to the accomplishment represented by the free historical subjectivity that one can discern the question that is posed when literature moves to dissolve all the distinctions by which we make sense of it, or to accomplish itself in a work that merely *is*, separate from all meaning, all relation to the world (EL 292, 220: cf. our Chapter 3). In *L'Entretien infini*, as the 'Note' continues, Blanchot proposes to articulate the sense of this question under the name of 'the neuter' (*le neutre*), located as a point of dissidence to all the categories of thought – the subject, identity, truth and the One (EI vii, xii). The close relationship between the philosophical questioning and the critical and historical research is already apparent in the more dramatic and 'literary' form of *L'Espace littéraire*. In the search for 'the essence of art', the writer discovers that the work begins not in the control over language, in the mastery of expression, but in the

---

19 See, for example, 'The Most Profound Question', 'The Great Refusal' or 'Atheism, Humanism and the Cry', among other texts in this volume.

experience of repetition (*recommencement*), in the absence of time, in belonging to 'the outside', in the discovery of the impersonal and neutral power to which writing and the image open (cf. EL VII.iii).[20] This thought provides the conditions of Blanchot's criticism, guiding the reading in advance, deciding what is most significant. These readings are not then purely textual, and do not have the same assumption as literary studies, when it considers itself as a form of 'research'. But such preconditions are necessary from the moment that one allows that modern literature can be understood as an historical event, and that it demands a reading that does not occupy the same conceptual space as the age from which it emerges.

---

20 The thought that gathers these terms together is studied in Chapter 4.

2 Poetic Solitude: Two Essays on Hölderlin

In order for Blanchot's work to be productively questioned and appropriated within literary studies, it is necessary first to decide to what extent his work belongs to this discipline. We will approach this question here in considering the example of the studies on Hölderlin. The first of these, 'The Sacred Word of Hölderlin', which is also the most comprehensive, illustrates the kinds of problem that would arise in the assessment of any of Blanchot's studies from within the discipline. The essay was first published in the journal *Critique*, in 1946, and then reproduced with only slight modifications in the collection *La Part du feu*. It presents itself in the first instance in the mode of the review article; the most noticeable modification in the book publication is the excision of the list of the works discussed from the head of the article – translations of some poems and articles on the poet, including the first translation into French of a commentary by Heidegger on Hölderlin, the essay entitled 'Wie wenn am Feiertage', published in an issue of the poetry journal *Fontaine*. Blanchot's essay does not limit itself to the function of the review article, but takes this occasion as the starting point for a reflection on Hölderlin's poetry as a whole. In this sense, the piece is ultimately closer to the critical genre of the author study. But it also diverges in many ways from the expectations to which this resemblance gives rise. Blanchot does not develop his interpretation as a step-by-step argument; nor does he examine alternate possible readings or consider possible obscurities or refractory passages. He only occasionally gives references, often does not clearly mark the transition from one poem to the next, and discusses no other commentators (except Heidegger). While such freedom from the conventions of the discourse can to some extent be attributed to the context of the public intellectual journal such as *Critique* (in contrast to the more highly formalized expectations of the university research publication), there are also more specific difficulties that suggest that the mode of presentation is the result of a conscious decision. One of the most general characteristics of Blanchot's critical and philosophical writing is the effacement of the hypotactic articulations that normally organize a principal argument and the stages of its demonstration. Assuming this is a deliberate strategy, it is questionable if an engagement with these texts is best served by converting them back into a series of theses. It may be more productive to begin by identifying the critical phenomenon upon which they reflect, and to read the essay as constructing the horizon within which this phenomenon should be seen. The critical problem is stated with particular clarity in this text:

> If one wishes to reflect on what is signified by the fact that the poem, that song exist, and if one claims to interrogate this fact from outside, this interrogation can only lead to Hölderlin, because here this question, experienced for itself and from within poetry, gave rise to the poem. (PF 121, 114)

These lines indicate the structure of the inquiry. Hölderlin's work as a whole is read as a meditation on the essence of poetry and on the task of the poet. But this work is not investigated purely for its own sake: the study takes place within the context of an interrogation of the existence of poetry that is pursued 'from the outside', that is to say, as a philosophical question, and that turns to Hölderlin, as one who has already encountered it from 'the inside', in the course of the production of a poetic work.

The double structure of the inquiry is reflected in the fluid and shifting line that separates interpretive and declarative moments of Blanchot's writing.[1] Take, for example, the following passage:

> There could be no poet, if the poet was not constantly aware of his impossibility, if he did not live this very impossibility. Let us consider more precisely what this impossibility signifies. This seems to be fundamental: the poet has to exist as the

---

[1] This technique is very characteristic of Blanchot's philosophical writing as well as the literary criticism; the problem is effectively sketched out in terms of the Blanchot–Levinas relation by Paul Davies in 'A Fine Risk: Reading Blanchot Reading Levinas', in *Re-reading Levinas*. Ed. Robert Bernasconi and Simon Critchley. Bloomington: Indiana UP, 1991, 201–208.

presentiment of himself, as the future of his own existence. He is not yet, but he has to be already as what he will be later on, in a 'not yet' that constitutes the essential of his mourning, his poverty and also his great wealth [. . .]

The poet only exists in anticipating the time of the poem: he is second in relation to the poem, of which he is nonetheless the creative power. (PF 121, 117)

Here, it is a matter of a contradiction that defines the poetic existence *in general* (that is, 'its essence and its law' (121, 117)), and not Hölderlin specifically. Indeed, the relation of the writer to the literary work is not a subject that is treated as such in Hölderlin's poetry, or even in his theoretical writings. It is, however, very much a concern of Blanchot's, one that returns at intervals throughout *La Part du feu*, under different guises. The formulations here are very close those advanced in the preceding essay, 'René Char'. Here, the assessment of a critical study on Char diverges briefly into some fundamental indications on reading and writing, in their relation to the work. It is the role of the poem, Blanchot writes, to transform both reader and writer, considered as individuals in the world, with the knowledge and the experience they have gathered from the world, into the reader and the writer proper to this singular work; in this sense, he writes, 'both the poet and the reader receive their existence from the poem, and are keenly aware of depending upon this song to come, this reader to become, for their very existence' (PF 104, 99).[2]

We need to recognize, then, that the claim at this point is not to represent the meaning of Hölderlin's work. Rather, it is to recapitulate the critic's own theses on the relation of writer and work: from this standpoint, it is possible to show how the same understanding comes to expression in the poet's work. A distinction of this form is constantly at work in Blanchot's readings. Let us develop a little the elements of a reading that underlies its deployment here. In Hölderlin, Blanchot suggests, this 'delay' in the poetic existence is apparent in

---

2   The theme returns in greater detail in 'Literature and the Right to Death', in which the temporal paradoxes of the act of writing are explored via the appropriation of a passage from Hegel (cf. PF 295ff): and it reappears, reproducing the formulations from these texts on Hölderlin and Char, in *L'Espace littéraire* (cf. EL 301–303). On Blanchot's discourse on writer, reader and work, see our Chapter 5.

the recurrence of the verbs *harren* (to persevere) and *ahnen* (to intuit something that is imminent):

> *Ich harrte, ich harrte,* this word constantly recurs to express the anguish and the sterility of waiting, as the word *ahnen* indicates its worth and potential, since it is this existence always to come of the poet that makes possible any future, and that maintains history firmly in the perspective of the 'tomorrow' that is richer in sense. [. . .] (PF 125, 117)

The mood of anticipation that is referred to here appears very often in Hölderlin. In both of Hölderlin's first two major works, the epistolary novel *Hyperion*, and the tragic drama *Empedokles*, the protagonist combines a religious or metaphysical intuition of the whole of nature, with a political vision of a possible reformation of the political and the social order. In 'Archipelagus', the long poem narrating the rise and fall of ancient Greek civilization, the Greek islands are depicted as languishing without the praise and the honour conferred by the temples, songs and cities of the past; and at the conclusion of the poem, the imminent return of the 'spirit of Nature' and the concomitant reawakening of the human soul is announced, a vision emblematically concentrated, as often, in the anticipation of the festival day (*Festtag*).

Through these and other versions, then, the poems are filled with a sense of the possibility of a historical transformation, and increasingly, of a religious transformation, a coming renewal of the bonds between man and divinity. Blanchot's reading can be contrasted with many studies of Hölderlin in that it concerns not so much the content of this expectation – the political ideals linked to the French revolution or the prophetic vision, the announcement of the 'coming gods' – but the fact of the expectation itself, considered as a distinctive mode of being, and its association with the existence of the poet. This kind of an approach does not need to be seen as a digression from the historical and religious themes of the poems towards a 'self-referential' meaning. It simply means that a reflection on the role of poetry is recognized as an integral part of the development of these themes: if this questioning is missed, then the poems would be reduced to a kind of versified commentary on political events and religious beliefs.

At the textual level, this interpretation can be justified by the representation of the poet himself. In 'An die Deutschen' ('To the

Germans'), the poet speaks of wandering (*irren*) through the land, with the sense of being present in 'the workshop of the creative spirit', conscious of something happening, and yet unable to say precisely what, divided between the exhilaration provoked by the signs of change, and conflicting feelings of impatience and doubt, and looking forward to the moment when doubt will be silenced before the 'divine day' (or divine light, *himmlische Tag*). At the end of the poem, the poet still abides by the 'cold shore' of his own time, no longer recognizing the contemporaries, a solitary voice that finds no echo. The same mood of solitude and anticipation appears in the closely related poem 'Rousseau', where the French thinker appears as an allegorical figure: he is the one who reads in the signs of his own time changes that are to come, prophesying 'the coming gods', but just for this reason, he encounters only incomprehension, and wanders endlessly in search of rest (*'gleich den Unbegrabenene, irrest du/ Unstet und suchest Ruh und niemand/ Weiß den bescheidenen Weg zu weisen'*).[3]

In a straightforward representational sense, anticipation is a projection, in imagination, towards a not yet given state of affairs, considered as capable of arriving independent of the imagining subject. In the interpretation, however – suggested in Hölderlin, spelled out by Blanchot – the anticipatory projection changes its sense: it becomes a response to something which is already there, but which has not yet come to clarity, which does not of itself have the necessary force of existence, and requires the poet's attention to show itself. 'All of Hölderlin's work', Blanchot writes, 'testifies to the awareness of an anterior power, beyond both the gods and men, which prepares the universe to be an integral whole' (PF 122, 119). A poem written as part of Hölderlin's work on *Empedocles*, entitled 'Nature and Art, or Saturn and Jupiter', can orient us in understanding what is designated here by this 'anterior power'. In the allegorical construction of the poem, Jupiter corresponds to 'Art', the word here having the wider sense of human arts and skills in general. Jupiter is condemned for having thrust Saturn, 'the sacred father' (*der heilige Vater*) – representing 'Nature' – into the underworld (*der Abgrund*). Jupiter rules high in the day, his law prevails, and he rests in his glory, but the

---

3   Citations from Hölderlin are taken from *Gesammelte Werke*. Ed. Hans Jürgen Balmes. München: Carl Hanser, 1990.

'singers' remember this first injustice. Saturn, the poem declares, was 'greater' than Jupiter – 'even though he gave no commands, and was named by no mortal' (*wenn schon/ Er kein Gebot aussprach und ihn der/ Sterblichen keiner mit Namen nannte*). Just as Jupiter's lightning bolt comes from the clouds, so he owes his 'immortal arts of mastery' (*unsterbliche Herrscherkünste*) to Saturn. The poem demands that Jupiter – and therefore, human art, power and mastery – no longer disavow its origin in Saturn (or 'nature'), and allow the poets to name 'the elder' before all gods and men (*Und gönn es ihm, dass ihn vor allen,/ Göttern und Menschen, der Sänger nenne*).

In this poem, it is the poets who recall Saturn, and who look forward to the moment when the just order will be restored. One finds something similar in 'As on the Festival Day' ('Wie wenn am Feiertage . . . '), the poem commented on by Heidegger. Here, the same anterior moment is present as 'Nature', which is said to be 'older than the times/ and above the gods of west and east' (*älter denn die Zeiten/ Und über die Götter des Abends und Orients*). In his commentary, Heidegger cautions against reading the poem with pre-existing conceptions of what is meant by 'Nature' in mind; the meaning of the term, he insists, has to be determined out of this poem alone.[4] It is nature, the poem tells us, that raises and educates the poets, in 'a light embrace', and in turn, the poets maintain the memory of nature, even when 'at times of the year', it seems to sleep, to be absent from the skies, from the plants, from the peoples (these 'times of the year', Heidegger suggests, should be understood as historical periods). During this period, the poets mourn, but their solitude and abandonment is not without hope: 'They seem to be alone, but they continue to anticipate (*ahnen*)/ For anticipating, she [Nature] rests too' (*Sie scheinen allein zu sein, doch ahnen sie immer/ Denn ahnend ruhet sie auch*). For this reason, it is the poets who prepare the moment of return, the moment that the poem itself then announces, in dramatic lines:

> But now the day breaks! I waited, and I saw it coming/
> And what I saw, may the Sacred be my word
> (*Jetzt aber tagt's! Ich harrt und sah es kommen,/*
> *Und was ich sah, das Heilige sei mein Wort.*).

---

4   *Elucidations of Hölderlin's Poetry*. Trans. Keith Hoeller. Amherst, NY: Humanity Books, 2000, 78–79.

For Heidegger, 'the sacred' here is a new and more original understanding of what is named by 'nature': 'in awakening, nature reveals its own essence as the sacred'.[5] Elements of Heidegger's language and interpretation are clearly present in Blanchot's text, but he does not make any attempt to defend or modify Heidegger's claims at the philosophical level.[6] The essay is more concerned to identify a field of meanings gathered around this term 'the sacred' in Hölderlin's poetry, and in so doing, to clarify the sense in which the poetic activity is here understood. What is named by 'the sacred', Blanchot suggests, is precisely this moment at which the daylight breaks:

> The sacred is the light (*le jour*): not the light of day as opposed to night, nor the celestial light, nor the infernal fire that Empedocles will seek. It is the light, and yet anterior to the light, and always anterior to itself, a light before the light (*un avant-jour*), a clarity before clarity. We come closest to this light in reflecting on the moment of waking, the infinitely distant moment of the break of day, which is also that which is most inner, more interior than all interiority. (PF 124, 121)

The 'sacred' is what is anterior to the light, not the darkness, but the very moment of beginning, that is subsumed by the light in which things are familiar to us. For Blanchot, this sense of an opening, an 'orient', is at the centre of Hölderlin's thought: he suggests analogies with a number of moments in other poems – with the movement 'to set out' (*aufbrechen*) to see the 'open' in 'Bread and Wine' ('Brot und Wein'), and with the gods who dwell above the light in 'Homecoming' ('Heimkunft'): one can see something similar in the awakening of spring in 'Der gefesselte Strom', in the source of the Rhine in 'Der Rhein', and in the poets themselves in their vocation to awaken the people, in 'Dichterberuf'.

---

5   Ibid., 80.
6   In Heidegger's interpretation, 'nature' and 'the sacred' are recognized as naming the being of beings: 'nature' in Hölderlin signifies that which 'grants to all real entities the open space within which the real as such can first appear'. ('*Die Natur . . . [verschenkt] allem Wirklichen die Lichtung, in deren Offenes hinein alles zu erscheinen vermag, was ein Wirkliches ist*') *Elucidations of Hölderlin's Poetry*, 81–82, translation slightly modified.

In each case what is depicted here is the movement of a beginning, prior to the stable and established order of things, the order symbolized by the rule of Jupiter in 'Nature and Art'. It is in this context, Blanchot proposes, that one has to understand the demand under which the poet stands in Hölderlin. The anterior light is evanescent, easily consumed in its own infinity: the poet's language is needed because it has the definiteness, the rigour that can preserve the relation to the sacred and make it into a foundation; 'the essence of language' for Hölderlin is 'to remain, if only as a trace, to be the foundation for that which remains, to establish "between day and night something true"' (PF 126, 124 the last lines are cited from the poem 'Germania'; on this reference, see below).

Before the poem, the light is the most obscure of all. As the origin of visibility, the pure beginning of what is to appear, it is the most profound mystery – and also the most terrifying: it is the unjustified, from which justification has to be drawn, the incommunicable and undiscovered which is, as such, also that which opens and which, through the rigor of poetic language, will in the end reveal itself. [...]

The poem, through its language, leads that which is unfounded to become foundation: it allows the abyss of the light to become the light which makes things appear and which constructs (130–131, 124–126).[7]

This passage illustrates the proximity to the text that characterizes Blanchot's critical style: the distance of the commentary that says something *about* the poem gives way to a 'repetition' of the poetic thought, in which the distance between the critical text and the words of the poet is no longer visible. It is important to see, however, that such claims are still based in a reading. Let us briefly recall some of the texts to which the passage alludes. As we have already seen in 'Nature

---

7 'Avant le poème, le jour est ce qu'il y a de plus obscur. Origine de la transparence, commencement pur de ce qui va jaillir, il est le mystère le plus profond – et aussi le plus effrayant: il est l'injustifié, à partir de quoi il faut prendre justification, l'incommunicable et l'indécouvert qui est aussi ce qui s'ouvre et, par la fermeté de la parole poétique, va devenir à la fin ce qui se découvre. [...] Le poème, par la parole, fait que ce qui est infondé devient fondement, que l'abîme du jour devient le jour qui fait surgir et qui construit'.

and Art or Saturn and Jupiter', the poets are placed under the rule of Saturn or 'Nature'. At the end of the poem, however, the condemnation of Jupiter is qualified: the poet will acknowledge Jupiter, now referred to as 'the wise master', as soon as Jupiter himself acknowledges Saturn. The word of Jupiter (the figure of 'Art'), in this positive incarnation, 'announces what is concealed in the sacred twilight' (*was die heilige Dämmerung birgt, verkundet*). When Jupiter's word no longer claims to be an autonomous utterance, but gives shape and definition to what glimmers in the half-light of Saturn's domain, then it corresponds precisely to the movement of poetry, such as Blanchot here reconstructs it (on the basis of Hölderlin's language and motifs): the poem is the making explicit, the un-concealment of what is present but obscure, or unformed. The metaphor for this act that is used here, the transition from the 'abyss of the light' to 'the light which makes things appear and constructs', is derived from the first two stanzas of the elegy 'Homecoming' ('Heimkunft'). The poem begins in the chaotic and mixed condition of the '*helle Nacht*' ('pale night') preceding the morning in the Alps, when the inhabitants of the valley are still in darkness, even as the light appears in the peaks. The stormbird (*Gewittervogel*) knows that it is time (*merkt die Zeit*) and calls the day to impose itself (*ruft den Tag*). Then the light that 'gleams and disappears', that is still unformed (*jung an Gestalt*), gathers density and, thanks to the intercession of a figure of the divine dwelling 'above the light', becomes the familiar clouds and breeze of a gentle and restorative spring: 'once again a life begins, grace unfolds as before, and the present spirit comes' (*jetzt wieder ein Leben beginnt,/ Anmut bluhst wie einst, and gegenwärtiger Geist kömmt*). The connection with the thought of poetry is suggested at the end of the poem, which speaks of the gifts soon to be granted by the divinity, and the anxieties (*die Sorgen*) of the poet as to how this divinity should be named and celebrated, since there are no sacred names (*es fehlen heilige Namen*). The poet, then, locates himself at the crucial moment of the beginning, and the perils attendant upon his task are prefigured in the 'successful' transition to the day instituted by the god in the opening stanzas. The sense that the poem accomplishes a beginning, that it grants a foundation, is also expressed in the hymn 'Germania', a poem to which Blanchot often refers. The dramatic situation is here again that of poetic anticipation. Renouncing his fascination for the (Greek) past, the poet resolves to remain with his own land and endure with it the state of tense expectancy in which he finds it: the prospect of the stormy sky signifies also the imminence of the new historical revelation of the divine that Hölderlin foresees. Then, shifting from a lyrical to an allegorical mode, the poem imagines an eagle coming across the Alps from the east, bringing the word from the gods to the German land, here represented by a young priestess of great faith, wrapped in a somnolent state (a little like the domain of Saturn). The eagle calls upon the priestess to 'drink in the morning air' – again the moment of dawn, as in 'Heimkunft' – and to name what is before her:

> No longer may the mystery
> Remain the unspoken,
> After it has been long concealed
> Modest reserve is proper to mortals
> And most of the time it is wise
> thus to speak of gods
> But where the gold is more abundant than pure springs
> And when the fury in the sky is in earnest,
> Between day and night
> One time there must appear something true.
> Three times you transcribe it,
> Nonetheless unspoken, as it is there,
> Innocent, it must remain.[8]

Here Hölderlin's poem ('Germania') anticipates and evokes the poem that is still to come, envisaged in the form of the words of the priestess. The poetic power of her words lies in their ability to name the 'mystery' in a way that also preserves its distance. It is in this sense, too, that the poetic utterance is still to come: it is not assimilated into an institution of understanding or culture, but retains the futural,

---

8   The translation aims simply to give the prose meaning: the word 'innocent' in the last line is a nominalized adjective, referring to and addressing the priestess. *'Nicht länger darf Geheimnis mehr/ Das Ungesprochene bleiben,/ Nachdem es lange verhüllt ist;/ Denn Sterblichen geziemet die Scham,/ Und so zu reden die meiste Zeit,/ Ist weise auch, von Göttern./ Wo aber überflüssiger, denn lautere Quellen,/ Das Gold und Ernst geworden ist der Zorn an dem Himmel,/ Muss zwischen Tag und Nacht/ Einmal ein Wahres erscheinen./ Dreifach umschreibe du es,/ Doch ungesprochen auch, wie es da ist,/ Unschuldige, muss es bleiben.'*

annunciatory character which Blanchot sees as essential to the poetic.[9] The words of the priestess mark the historical turning point that the poem ('Germania') begins in anticipating: in announcing the mystery that has been long concealed, she inaugurates a new era, the new historical world that is celebrated in the next and final stanza.

In assembling some of the implied references, we can see the sense in which Blanchot's text remains critical, despite the appearance some passages have of being pure affirmations. The problematic relationship of Blanchot's work to literary criticism cannot be grasped at the formal level, in terms of its non-conformity to the expectations of verification and argument that are customary in a specific discipline or professional discourse. Certainly, the essay does not employ the didactic style of argument and demonstration, but it is still based on an understanding that could in principle be developed with the differentiation and the detail proper to writing within the disciplines. The problem is deeper, and has to be addressed in terms of the 'proximity' of text and critic that we have noted. The work of the poet is not isolated as an 'object' of study from which the language of the study maintains itself at a formal distance. The reconstruction of Hölderlin's thought of the poetic is not proposed as a set of ideas or poetic motifs, proper to one particular poet, one particular historical period, located within a total horizon of research (e.g. literature, literary history, modern European literature, etc.). The assumption is that the possibility of the poetic has been questioned and discovered anew in Hölderlin's poetry, and that the critical task is to restate what comes to light there, to articulate it from outside the language specific to the poet; hence the gesture of identification implied in the placement of the passage from 'Germania' as the epigraph to *La Part du feu*.

This stance remains implicit in the rhetoric of the essay that we have been reading, but it will become clearly visible if we turn now to 'Literature and the Original Experience', the final essay in *L'Espace littéraire*, in which Blanchot provides something close to a synthetic restatement of the historical and philosophical themes developed in the course of this work. At its very conclusion, in a brief and rather

---

9   This dimension of the poetic is particularly developed in relation to the poetry of René Char: in addition to the text 'René Char' in *La Part du feu*, see the later text entitled 'The Beast of Lascaux', now in *Une Voix venue d'ailleurs*. Paris: Gallimard, 2002.

oblique coda, the essay turns to Hölderlin (EL 330–333). This discussion is an abbreviated and modified version of an earlier text, published in 1951, entitled 'Madness *par excellence*'.[10] In this first form, this commentary prolongs the inquiry commenced in 'The Sacred Word of Hölderlin': there is the same concern with Hölderlin as the 'poet of poetry', the same tendency towards a synthetic understanding of the work on the hermeneutic assumption that each text is explicated by all the others. As such, like the earlier text, it is essentially interpretive and critical in its aims, if somewhat idiosyncratic in its procedure. The situation is different, however, when this commentary is extracted from its original context and re-located as the conclusion to *L'Espace littéraire*. Now it becomes very apparent that Blanchot's philosophical exposition understands itself as the appropriation and the making explicit of what Hölderlin discovers: there is no longer the objectivity and neutrality that is implied by commentary as a contribution to knowledge or understanding.

Where the first essay on Hölderlin ranges freely over the poet's work as a whole, this second study consists primarily in an exegesis of the elegy 'Bread and Wine' ('Brot und Wein'). As a result, there is a stronger emphasis on Hölderlin's religious – and philosophical historical thought, of which this poem is one of the most important statements. For Hölderlin, the modern era is the time of the absence of the gods, of the withdrawal of the divinity which, according to his heterodox and syncretic conception, was present in Greece no less than in early Christianity. The question of the significance of poetry takes on its sense within this historical vision. '*Wozu Dichter in dürftiger Zeit?*', the poem asks, what need is there for poets in the time of distress? Hölderlin can therefore illustrate the claim developed by Blanchot in the earlier part of this essay that the modern poet can no longer merely produce new works, but has also to decide what poetry is and if it exists at all (cf. our Chapter 1). In Hölderlin, this challenge is met through an affirmation of the 'original' function of poetry, as the naming and praising of 'the higher' and 'the highest' (cf. 'Der Prinzessin Auguste von Homburg', 'Dichterberuf'). The

---

10 'La Folie par excellence', *Critique*, 45, 1951, 99–118. The essay was not collected in any of Blanchot's volumes of criticism. It is available in English in *The Blanchot Reader*. Ed. Michael Holland. Oxford: Blackwell, 1995, 110–128.

recollection of this function, however, only exacerbates the contradiction before which the poet stands, now that the 'father has turned his face away from men and mourning has rightly begun on the earth' ('Brot und Wein', stanza viii). When the divine presence that poetry once announced and celebrated has withdrawn from the collective, the poet endures a condition of enforced idleness, and has nothing to do but wait, in solitude (*so zu harren, ohne Freunde*).

As this poem shows, however, this is not a purely negative or tragic predicament. The meaning of the situation is modified by the understanding of the historical nature of divine revelation, announced by the poem as a whole. The poet endures the solitude of waiting, without the gathering of community and place that was present in the ancient world (stanzas iv to vi): but it is not at all times that man is capable of enduring the presence of the divine (*Nur zu Zeiten erträgt göttliche Fülle der Mensch*). Moreover, 'error helps, like sleep, and need and the night make strong' (stanza vii).[11] These terms name the mode of being that corresponds to the absence of the gods, and that preserves the relation to the gods in their absence. They have the positive sense of memory, of preparation and of anticipation (*l'attente*), and should be understood by contrast with a kind of facile accommodation or a falling into a condition of mere forgetting. The strange phrase 'error helps' (*das Irrsal hilft*) is to be understood in this sense: the basic meaning of this expression is preserved better by the French *l'erreur*, signifying first of all the wandering movement of a migration without definite goal – although in Blanchot's commentary, at least, there is a deliberate play between the spatial sense (associated more with the verb *errer*) and the epistemological meaning (*l'erreur*): in this way, the absence of fixed location, of a dwelling or homeland, is superimposed upon the condition of not being in the truth.[12] This sense is specifically related to the poet in the final lines of this stanza: here, negating or at least qualifying the initial expression of futility and despair ('What use the poet?', *Wozu Dichter?*), Hölderlin writes

---

11 '*Denn nicht immer vermag ein schwaches Gefäß sie zu fassen,/ Nur zu Zeiten erträgt göttliche Fülle der Mensch. Traum von ihnen ist drauf das Leben. Aber das Irrsal/ Hilft, wie Schlummer, und stark machet die Not und die Nacht.*' ('Brot und Wein', stanza vii).
12 The motif appears in a number of Hölderlin's poems: cf. 'Der Main', 'Rousseau', 'Dem Allbekannten', 'Der Ister', and reappears in a somewhat different context with the disciples in 'Patmos' who are dispersed on their separate paths after the death of Jesus.

that, after all, the poets are like the priests of Dionysus who 'moved from land to land in holy night' (*wie des Weingotts heilige Priester/ Welche von Lande zu Land zogen in heiliger Nacht*). The solitude of the poet, his lack of a place, in the sense of a function within the community ('Wozu . . . ?'), signifies also that he remains at a distance from the factitious permanence of the world, such as it is; precisely because the poets do not belong to the existing order, their language can open up the place – that is, it can have the foundational role that Hölderlin assigns to poetry. This is the sense of the other part of the comparison: the poet is also like Dionysos (or his priests) in that poetry, too, can awaken the people to a higher mode of being, as in 'The Poet's Vocation', or can found culture and cultivation, as in 'The Only One' ('Der Einzige', where Dionysos is given this function).

Up to a certain point, then, Blanchot continues to occupy the mode of commentary. Indeed, in 'Madness *Par Excellence*', the text does not go beyond this point: the reading of 'Brot und Wein', supported by a network of correspondences with other poems, shows that for, Hölderlin, the poet, in living the 'time of distress', the moment of separation, prepares and announces the return of the gods.[13] In its repetition in *L'Espace littéraire*, however, this commentary passes without transition into Blanchot's own concluding restatement of the sense of the poetic activity:

> The proper, the force, the risk of the poet is to have his dwelling there where god is absent, in this region without truth. The time of distress designates this time, in all times, which is proper to art but which, at the historical moment when the gods are absent and the world of truth vacillates, emerges in the work as the concern in which it has its reserve, which menaces it, makes it present and visible. (EL 331, 246)

---

13 The religious thought implied in this interpretation is developed in greater detail in 'The Itinerary of Hölderlin' (the last of the 'Annexes', in *L'Espace littéraire*). In the late letters and his writings on Sophocles, Blanchot argues, Hölderlin formulates the demand upon the poet in the time of the absence of the gods: on the one hand, he has to avoid the temptation of the divine, which draws one away from the world, but on the other hand, he has also to avoid the purely secular existence. Rather, he has to occupy the 'between' (*l'entre-deux*). It is worth noting that, although this text returns very much to the mode of commentary, *l'entre-deux* then reappears as part of Blanchot's own philosophical vocabulary in *L'Entretien infini*.

These words resonate with the poems of Hölderlin that we have been discussing, but they also have a wider significance. This concluding section of *L'Espace littéraire* serves to indicate a response to the *historical* question to which the essay – and the book – as a whole addresses itself: 'why is it that, at the moment at which history contests it, art tends to become essential presence?' (The question is posed at the end of the first section of 'Literature and the Original Experience', EL 292, 220 and then again at the conclusion, EL 329, 245) The answer is that it is precisely at the moment at which it is no longer absorbed in the role granted it by the most essential concerns of the society that poetry/art is able to discover its true sense. The significance of the poetic possibility had been disguised when it was the medium by which the divine is present to the collective, and excluded entirely when human society came to understand itself in terms of 'the work of history'. At this moment, poetry and art are relegated to the domain of the aesthetic. But at this moment, too, poetry (or art) emerges as the concern in which the work has its 'reserve' (cf. EL 308–311, 231-233). For Blanchot, 'the time of distress' in which the poet finds himself names 'the time proper to art at all times'. The 'force, the power, the risk' of the poet lies in the ability to inhabit the empty time of the absence of the gods, to dwell in the region without truth, to endure the privation of centre and domain that is designated as 'error' (*l'erreur*). At this point, we have to understand that this condition is not solely a consequence of a particular historical conjuncture, something with which the poet has more or less lucidly and courageously to come to terms. Rather, it names the positive *possibility* represented by poetry, that which art and poetry alone are able to accomplish. It is in these terms, then – which the very last pages of Blanchot's essay sketch out – that one can say that poetry still has a meaning for us. Because the poet belongs to 'the time of distress', this time anterior to the time of action in the world, language is not only an instrument of understanding and negotiating, but also offers the possibility of beginning: hence the poetic work can be the first light, the 'now' of the day that rises. Hence Blanchot can use the language of Hölderlin to affirm the positive character of the poetic work as he understands it: the work is the first moment of light that precedes the day, *le point du jour qui précéderait le jour* (EL 305, 229).

To understand the sense these claims have *for Blanchot* will require more extensive study of his work.[14] For the moment, our intention is primarily to clarify the relation between the critical and the literary text, in this case Hölderlin. One can see Blanchot's critical writing – its 'poetic' character, its use of literary figures and narratives, the erasure of the boundary between text and criticism – as a solution to a limit that criticism encounters in dealing with certain kinds of literary work. A poetry that dedicates itself to 'nature', 'the sacred', 'the highest' – and which claims moreover that it is uniquely poetry that sustains this relation – provides criticism with a stark alternative. Either it can remain within the discursive field of research, and then the truth of poetry (such as it appears in the poem) is *a priori* bracketed, reduced to the status of a documented representation, an object of research in the history of ideas, and in the political and theological history from which the poetry emerges; or, on the other hand, instead of determining what these terms mean in their contemporary context, the critic can try to understand what they are pressed into service to name; but in this case the commentary remains 'poetic' from the standpoint of the discipline. The fact that the language of Blanchot's essays on Hölderlin continues to have a recurrent subterranean presence in his own later reflections indicates that these are among the texts in which he encounters this alternative and decides for the latter possibility.

---

14 See Chapter 5 of this study.

3 Mallarmé and Modern Poetics

I

Essays devoted to Mallarmé appear in each of Blanchot's first four volumes of criticism, and in each case, these are among the texts in which the most general questions posed by the critical work are addressed. These are not a series of studies covering different areas of the poet's work: rather, in each of these essays, by different paths, Blanchot approaches the idea of poetry that is proposed by Mallarmé's work. In studying them in comparison one can see the changes in the style proper to each of the phases to which they belong. More importantly, one can also track the continuity of an inquiry that is sustained through the phases of Blanchot critical work, as well as the close connections that link the studies on Mallarmé to Blanchot's own poetics.

The texts collected in Blanchot's first collection, entitled *Faux Pas*, are mostly brief reviews, written specifically in response to contemporary publications. But already here, the texts on Mallarmé have greater independence from their occasion than most others in the collection, and show certain basic orientations that will remain consistent in Blanchot's later criticism. The first of the three, 'The silence of Mallarmé', a review of the biography by Henri Mondor, takes its point of departure from the personal itinerary of the poet.

> Mallarmé was conscious of his work when he was little more than an adolescent. At the age of 23, not only does he begin to write '*Hérodiade*', but he is already in possession of his crystalline system, from which all facility is absent, a practice of ordering words according to new relations, by reflexion, research, rigorous intuitions. More than this, he discerns that this poetics, based on a will to formal perfection, is something so prodigiously impossible that its realization would amount to the creation of the universe. To him, the written work seems to have

the weight, the mystery, the power of the world. It is something that could not be. (FP 126–127, 100–101)

The poetic activity in Mallarmé is not oriented towards the production of discrete individual works: it involves a 'system', a 'practice', a 'research', terms implying an ongoing investigation in the course of which initial intuitions are determined and take on their full sense. This research is set in motion with the conception of a future work, first sketched out by Mallarmé in the letters of 1866–1867. The creation of the poem that is here envisaged is analogous to the creation of the universe because the poem, too, has the 'weight, the mystery, the power' of something that exists in itself, without being governed by prior rules or conventions. In each of the essays that follows, Blanchot returns to this claim: far from viewing it as a hyperbole or a literary myth, he places it at the centre of Mallarmé's accomplishment: this conception, he writes here, allows Mallarmé to approach 'the art of writing in its purity' (127, 101).

In *Faux Pas*, Mallarmé's idea of art is often invoked as a measure by which the shortcomings of contemporary work can be seen. In 'Mallarmé and the Art of the Novel', for example, this conception is proposed as a model for 'a definition of the art of the novel' (198, 166), and in several essays, it is favourably contrasted with the dominance of realism in contemporary novelistic practice.[1] This use of Mallarmé is much less marked in later texts, where one does not find the same kind of prescriptive rhetoric nor the direct, polemical engagement with contemporary literary production. What is retained, however, is the use of Mallarmé's work, more than any actual descriptive term, as a reference point to indicate a distinctive tendency in modern literature. At the end of 'Mallarmé and the Art of the Novel', Joyce is mentioned as a possible example of the novel written on Mallarméan principles (204, 177). In 'The Secret of Melville', Melville's *Moby Dick* is considered as an illustration of Mallarmé's conception of the artwork: 'it seeks to be a total book, not only expressing a complete human experience but giving itself as written equivalent to the universe' (282, 239). Blanchot adds that the evocation of this ideal does not have to be correlated to literal

---

1   See, in particular, 'The Recent Novel' ('Le Jeune roman') and 'The Enigma of the Novel', FP 217–226, 183–191.

comprehensiveness: 'one has the same impression before the tales of Edgar Poe as before Joyce's *Ulysses*, before the sonnets of Gérard de Nerval as before Lautréamont's *Maldoror*' (283, 240).

Already in these early texts, then, Mallarmé serves to designate a tendency that marks modern literature more generally, by which works have a more concentrated sense of their own character as poetry, as literature (cf. EL 292–293, 219–220). There is historical justification for such a point of view, since, to a considerable extent, the tendency is propagated in more or less direct contact with Mallarmé's work and thought. The influence of Mallarmé on modern poetry and poetics is immense, and still awaits comprehensive study. In France, his poetics was sustained and redoubled through the work of Valéry whose writings on literature, while more accessible and more widely read than Mallarmé, present themselves as the prolongation of his innovations; in England, Mallarmé's ideas were transmitted by Symons' work on the symbolist school and subsequently by the acknowledged influence of this school on the most noted modern poets, including Yeats, Eliot and Pound; and in Germany, Mallarmé's work was mediated and advocated in a more programmatic way by Stefan George who, like Wilde, Yeats and many others, was present in the famous informal lectures and meetings held at the poet's apartment towards the end of his life. It seems reasonable to assume that if the works of this notoriously obscure writer have had such great resonance, it may well have been because he gives expression to an impulse that has deeper origins than his own direct and indirect influence. Mallarmé can be seen, then, not merely as an example of this tendency, but also as a key to its interpretation, the one who, by his prose, letters, and poems, provides its most revealing expression.[2]

---

2   The use of Mallarmé as a paradigmatic figure places Blanchot's work in proximity to literary-historical studies seeking to disentangle the cluster of factors that converge around the ideas of art and poetry in symbolist and modernist discourse. Recent studies of the historical and cultural significance of modern poetics for which Mallarmé appears as an exemplary figure include Bertrand Marchal, *Lire le Symbolisme*. Paris: Dunod, 1993, and Pascal Durand, *Poésies de Stéphane Mallarmé*, Paris, Gallimard, coll. Foliothèque, 1998. By their interest in the situation of the work within the culture of nineteenth century France, these studies are close to the prevailing style in English-language literary criticism (in contrast with the tradition of Mallarmé scholarship, which has tended to be more exegetic and philosophical).

Certain tensions in these earliest texts assume greater significance when considered in this light. In the passage above, for example, the intention underlying Mallarmé's 'practice of ordering words' is said to consist in the 'will to formal perfection'. If this is taken as the starting point, the guiding trait from which Mallarmé's enterprise is to be understood, then it would seem legitimate to see the literary tendency that his work exemplifies as having its philosophical presuppositions in idealism. The notion of 'autonomy' (as in 'aesthetic autonomy' or the 'autonomy of the literary sphere'), often used to identify what is central to this tendency, encourages such an interpretation. The autonomy of the literary work can readily be understood as realizing and demonstrating the potential autonomy of consciousness from its contingency and situatedness. At points Mallarmé expressly uses the term 'idealism' to describe his own practice (in the prose text, 'Crise de vers', for example, in which, moreover, the goal attributed to the poem is to liberate 'the pure notion'), and it is generally acknowledged that his thought owes something to the influence of Hegel, even if the precise extent of this filiation is a long running question in the scholarship.[3] One could see elements of the language of idealism in the early stages of Blanchot's reflection – as when, in early essays on the novel, he opposes the *inner* necessity of the work based solely on the dictates of imagination to the *external* necessity of an art based on verisimilitude (cf. FP 225–226, 191).

There are also statements, in this same text, however, which point in quite a different direction. Already in the passage we have cited, the suggestion that the written work would have the creation of a universe as its hyperbolic measure diverges from the finite perfection suggested by the idea of form. A little later, it is suggested that the pursuit of poetry leads Mallarmé into something resembling a mystical experience:

> Through the manipulation of words, indefinitely weighed and revised, [Mallarmé] gained access to the domain of essences and his vision came to resemble a spiritual vision, by the violence with which it solicited his entire life, drawing him away from the everyday world and exposing him to the most demanding

---

3   For a study of this question, arguing for a strong link, see Janine D. Langan, *Hegel and Mallarmé*. New York: University Press of America, 1986.

experiences. These experiences are of a remarkable character, and one cannot sufficiently meditate on the letters in which Mallarmé alludes to them. It seems at first glance no more than the fatigues of a mind prey to an unrealizable dream, exposed by its own excesses to sterility. In reality, what he suffers is of an entirely different nature. It resembles rather the sufferings endured by certain souls in the night of mysticism. One would have to say that, by an extraordinary effort of ascesis, Mallarmé had opened an abyss in himself; and yet his consciousness is not lost, but survives itself, grasps its solitude with a desperate clarity. (127, 101)

The biographical framework of 'The Silence of Mallarmé', with its narrative, reflective style, elides the transition between what, on closer examination, appear to be two quite different representations of the 'pure art of writing'. On the one hand, writing is identified with formal objectives such as totality and perfection; on the other hand, it appears as the instrument or the path of discovery, accomplished in the poet's existence as much as in the poem itself. Later in the text, Blanchot remarks that what is distinctive in Mallarmé, what separates him from the line of literary visionary experience, is that his trajectory is determined by the 'consciousness and the contemplation of words'; not from 'a verbal intoxication and fascination', but from the practice of 'a methodical arrangement of words' (128, 102). This remark seems to be intended to bring the two orientations of the text together. It would be precisely the practical, 'artisanal' activity, then, the meticulous concern with written expression, that precipitates the 'mystical' experience. But here this convergence is, at most, posed for future reflection.[4] The text does not elaborate on what is signified by this experience, nor how it clarifies or qualifies the demand of a total poetic creation, such as Mallarmé initially conceives it.

---

4 The essay on Mallarmé in *L'Espace littéraire*, first published in 1952, ten years after these brief pieces from *Faux Pas*, opens by reflecting on the 'astonishing' remarks from the letters referred to in the text above, linking an artisanal concern with language (*'en creusant le vers'*, *'le seul acte d'écrire'*) and an extreme experience, an encounter with nothingness and with the absence of the gods (cf. EL 37–38, 38–39).

Similar tensions can be observed in the next essay in *Faux Pas*, entitled 'Is Mallarmé's Poetry Obscure?' The point of departure of this text lies with a collection of commentaries on Mallarmé's poetry.[5] Once again, the review provides the occasion for a sketch of a more general reflection on Mallarmé's idea of poetry. Where in the previous text, the poem is considered as a project and an experience for the writer, here it is approached rather in terms of the challenge it poses to understanding and commentary. The consequence of Mallarmé's poetics is that the meaning of the poem is inseparably linked to its language. For this reason, the poem cannot possibly be reproduced in the form of a paraphrase.

> The first characteristic of poetic signification is that it is bound, without possible alteration, to the language that manifests it . . . The meaning of the poem is inseparable from all the words, all the movements, all the accents of the poem. It only exists within this ensemble and disappears as soon as one tries to separate it from the form that it has received. What the poem signifies coincides exactly with what it is [. . .] (135–136, 108)

The way in which the distinction of poetic language is here formulated is very close to certain of the texts of Paul Valéry. In his essays on poetry and aesthetics, Valéry ever again returns to the idea, transmitted with the force of an axiom by Mallarmé, that the language of poetry is essentially different from the language of comprehension. In many texts, Valéry maintains this distinction in terms of the particular signifying value acquired in poetry by words themselves, their sounds, accent, movement, identifying the poetic effect with what he calls the 'domain of sensibility that is governed by language'.[6] In Valéry, too, the impossibility of paraphrase is the measure of the poetic. 'To resume a thesis is to retain the essential of it. To summarize a work of art (or to replace it with a schema) is to lose the essential'.[7]

---

5 Charles Mauron, *Mallarmé l'obscur*. Paris: Denöel, 1941.
6 'Calepin d'un poète', in *Oeuvres*. Tome I. Paris: Gallimard, 1957, 1458.
7 'Leonardo et les philosophes', *Oeuvres*. Tome I, 1244. For more developed statements of the idea, see, among other texts, the essays 'Je disais quelquefois à Stéphane Mallarmé', 'Questions de poésie' and (especially) 'La Poésie et la pensée abstraite', in the same volume.

The main difference in Blanchot's version of this distinction is that what seems at first (as in Valéry) primarily a structural and descriptive determination of the poetic comes then to acquire metaphysical significance:

> In the poetic act, language ceases to be an instrument and shows itself in its essence, which is to found a world, to make possible the authentic dialogue that we are, and, as Hölderlin says, to name the gods. In other words, language is not only an accidental means of expression, a shadow allowing the invisible body to be seen, it also has an independent existence (*il est aussi ce qui existe en soi-même*), as an ensemble of sounds, of cadences, of numbers, and in this way, by the concatenation of forces that it figures, it reveals itself as the foundation of things and of human existence. (137, 109)

The contrast in register of the discussion, glided over in the preceding essay, is more striking here, in part because of the diverse texts that are being merged. The role of poetry is formulated in terms which reproduce very closely (though entirely without acknowledgement) certain of the theses of Heidegger's 1930 text 'Hölderlin and the Essence of Poetry'.[8] In the absence of the conceptual explications provided by Heidegger, and the close intertextual relation to Hölderlin's poetry in Heidegger's text, one may well find the emergence of this declaration out of the theoretical description of the characteristics of poetic language rather abrupt and insufficiently motivated. Moreover, the text seems undecided on the rhetoric of its own claims: at one moment, poetry is 'the foundation of things and of human reality'; at the next, it merely 'imposes *a momentary belief* in the sensuous power of words, their ability to come into contact with the depths of existence' (137, 110, my italics). It remains undecided, then, whether poetry is a genuine power of disclosure or whether it merely creates the effect of such a disclosure; indeed, the alternative is explicitly held open: Blanchot refers to 'this fact or illusion that language has an essential reality,

---

8 In 'Mallarmé and the Art of the Novel', the same theses of Heidegger are developed in somewhat more detail, though still without attribution; not even Hölderlin is mentioned in this text; instead Heidegger's theses are directly attributed to Mallarmé. (FP 199–201). This merging of Heidegger and Mallarmé reappears in *L'Espace littéraire*, as we will see; there, too, it is neither signalled nor explained.

a fundamental mission' ('*ce fait ou illusion que le langage a une réalité essentielle, une mission fundamentale*', 137, 110).

II

These early essays are helpful to approach Blanchot's critical writings, precisely because their conceptual means and orientation are still somewhat tentative in comparison with the later texts, which inhabit their own terrain of thought and language with such assurance that it is very difficult to locate a point of exteriority from which to initiate critical dialogue. In the tensions of the early texts, one can see the alternatives before which Blanchot's criticism stands at its outset, and hence the decision represented by the path it subsequently takes. One sees, for example, the points of proximity and distance in relation to existing critical discourse on modern poetics. In the first text, the notion of formal perfection of a self-sufficient structure of language is very close to what is generally understood by the idea of aesthetic autonomy; and in the second, the conception of literature in terms of a specific disposition of sign and meaning points in the direction of more recent literary–theoretical attempts to define the specificity of the 'object' of literary study. On the other hand, the texts combine this kind of 'technical' conception with what we can provisionally refer to – using loosely these far from precise terms – as a 'Romantic' or 'metaphysical' language: in the first case, the 'abyss' that is opened up in the self, in the process of writing; in the second, the 'depth of existence', which the poem is capable of evoking, and by virtue of which it is said to be able to give 'foundation' to a human world. The result is a somewhat different image of Mallarmé than that which is encouraged by many aspects of his production – the proto-modernist, innovatory stance (e.g. the support for free verse, the typographic experiments of 'Un Coup de dés'), the proximity to late nineteenth-century movements such as aestheticism and decadence, the interest in the cultural life and media phenomena of Parisian society, and so on. In Blanchot's readings, such tendencies, while not simply neglected, take on their sense in relation to the fact that, in reflecting upon the poetic act, Mallarmé is led to see anew what it means that we relate to the world through language. This revelation, announced and dramatized in the letters of 1866–1868, remains for Blanchot the centre around which the thought and the poetry turn. The essays in *Faux Pas* do little more than point towards this critical perspective; the more extended subsequent essays develop the presuppositions required for such an interpretation.

In its language and argument, 'The Myth of Mallarmé' in *La Part du feu* (an essay first published in periodical form in 1946) is closer to a more conventional theoretical exposition. The analysis is far more detailed and textual than in the brief essays of *Faux Pas*. The essay begins by suggesting that what is most distinctive and significant in Mallarmé has to be recovered from its reception history, which, in making the work known, has also fixed it in the form of the cult of aesthetic value. By these remarks, Blanchot distances his concerns from the historical connections of Mallarmé's poetry with aestheticism and formalism, connections which include his influence in the 1890s, in England (e.g. Wilde, the English reception of symbolism), as well as in France. In order to shift the perspective, Blanchot turns to the prose writings, suggesting that the demands that Mallarmé associates with poetry can be illuminated by the theoretical reflections on language in these texts.

What Mallarmé discovers in language, Blanchot suggests, is a destructive agency, the power to transpose the thing into its 'near disappearance' (*la merveille de transposer un fait de nature en sa presque disparition* as it is designated in the prose text 'Crise de vers'). Blanchot comments:

> The word can only have its meaning if it frees us of the object that it names: it has to spare us its presence, or 'le concret rappel'. Authentic language has not only a representative, but a destructive function. It causes to *disappear*, it makes the object absent, it annihilates it. (PF 37, 30)

Mallarmé's reflection upon language, Blanchot suggests, takes its point of departure in the functioning of language as a power of abstraction, its ability to replace the uniqueness of things with a universal concept. Language makes things disappear in the here and now of their presence, replacing them with a sign, which makes up for what it loses in concreteness with its gain in manipulability.[9] In language as we encounter it in the world, however, the distancing of

---

9   This analysis communicates closely with Blanchot's own reflection on language, as developed throughout *La Part du feu*, most comprehensively in 'Literature and the Right to Death' : cf. our Chapter 4.

'the thing' is provisional, and in general, barely noticed. The word supposes the absence of the referent, the thing in its presence, but at the moment at which it refers, the thing reappears in the form of a signification (PF 39, 31). In its everyday usage, then, language itself has no substantial existence: it is a mere function, vanishing into the thing that it signifies, comparable to the coin that is passed from hand to hand in a commercial transaction (to recall the metaphor Mallarmé uses in 'Crise de vers'). Poetic language, by contrast, is 'authentic' language because it allows language its own existence: that is to say, it allows the distantiation of reality (the operation proper to language) to subsist, to be present, against the pressure of things and meanings.

> In general, language is the possibility of destroying the world in order that it be re-created as meaning, as signified values; but in its creative form, it holds to the negative aspect of its task, and becomes a pure power of contestation and transfiguration. (44–45, 37)

The poetic qualities of language are a means of heightening and enabling the negation of reality, its 'contestation and transfiguration'. Sound and rhythm, for example, have their value in that they intervene in the movement of understanding, bringing the material presence of language into view, and with this also, the 'work' of negation that language performs:

> One understands why the essential language allows so great a place to what Valéry calls the physicality of language. Sounds, rhythm, number, all that has no importance in everyday language, now becomes the most important. The words need to be visible, they need a reality of their own, in order to interpose themselves between that which is (*ce qui est*) and that which they express. (39, 31)

By its stylization, its formal and material patterning, poetry places a barrier between language and 'that which is' – real things, in their presence. Mallarmé's poetics consists in a program for the integral accomplishment of this effect, in principle active in all poetry. In order to inhibit the reassertion of the presence of things, and consequently, the subordination of language, the poem has to become 'a flight of images, transitions of sense, rather than images', such that no definite signification can take command of the work – 'a rhythmical trajectory, in which what counts is the passage, the modulation' (41, 32 cf. also 69–70, 64). For this reason, too, the paradigm of such an art is writing and the book rather than voice or song:

> The book is the mode of language *par excellence*, because it preserves only its power of abstraction, of isolation, of transposition; because it separates from language all that remains of the contingency of real things, and finally because it separates language from man, from the one who speaks and hears: '*Impersonnifié, le volume, autant qu'on s'en sépare comme auteur, ne réclame approche de lecteur. Tel, sache, entre les accessoires humains, il a lieu tout seul: fait étant*'. (PF 43, 40)

The hyperbolic possibility that Mallarmé envisages under the name of 'the Work' (*l'Oeuvre*) is not the microcosm of the world, but rather the realization of its absence – 'the hollow space of this totality, its other side, its realized absence' (*le creux de cette totalité, son envers, son absence realisée*) (43, 36):

> Having discovered language as an exceptional power of absence and contestation, it is tempting to consider the absence of language as contained in its essence, and thus to see silence as the ultimate possibility of language. It is well known that this poet was haunted by silence. What has often been forgotten is that silence for him does not mark the failure of his dreams, no more than it represents an acquiescence to the ineffable, a gesture of renunciation in the face of poetic resources inferior to the ideal. Silence is always present, as the only demand worth accomplishing. But it is not the other of words: on the contrary, it is supposed by words, their secret intention, more even, the condition of language, assuming that to speak is to replace a presence by an absence and to pursue, through ever more fragile presences, an ever more accomplished absence. Silence only has such value because it is the highest degree of this absence,

which is the whole virtue of speech (itself a power of giving a meaning, of separating us from things in order to signify them). (42, 34)[10]

We can see how this analysis continues and elaborates the basic critical intervention sketched out in the early essays. The difference is that, in place of the metaphors of depth and obscurity deployed in the early texts, the claim for poetry is now justified in a more 'theoretical' style. Mallarmé's poetics does not represent a preference for a certain kind of aesthetic effect, such as coldness, distance or perfection. The thinking of 'the Work' – that is, of the immanence of the poem, its necessity, its absolute existence – begins with an interpretation of language, as the element of our relation to the world. The characteristic gestures identified with the poetics of Mallarmé – the 'impressionism', the attenuation of objects, their distancing into their *'presque disparition'*, the recognition of a poetic value to prose, the comparison of poetry to music, the insistence on the impersonality of the work, the emphasis on methods of suggestion, allusion or transposition (cf. the concluding passages of Mallarmé's 'Crise de vers'), the special importance given to the scriptural dimension of language – all of these features are here given their sense in terms of a fundamental poetic intention: the production of absence or of 'silence'.

One should note also the concern to distinguish this interpretation from religious or metaphysical ideas: silence is not 'the other of words', the ineffable, but rather the 'condition' of words, their possibility. At times the language of *La Part du feu* – for example, the reference to 'absolute absence' later in this text (PF 46, 40) – can seem to invoke a kind of negative metaphysical substance, which the poem would be naming or pointing toward. But Blanchot consistently dismisses any conception that would make the work the privileged access to a metaphysical truth.[11] Remaining within the terms of the text we have analyzed here, we can see that 'absence' does not signify

---

10 '*Qu'une moyenne étendue de mots, sous la comprehension du regard, se range en traits définitifs, avec quoi le silence*', 'Crise de vers', in *Igitur, Divagations, Un Coup de dés*. Preface by Yves Bonnefoy. Paris: Gallimard, 1976, 245.
11 Above all, through an ongoing polemic against symbolic interpretation. See, for example, 'The Secret of the Golem', in *Le Livre à venir*. Here, Blanchot affirms the immanence of the literary work, writing that: 'the beyond of the work is real only in the work, is nothing but the reality of the work itself' (LV 125, 90).

some pre-existing 'substance', nor even a substantial non-substance, a void that would be present in some way. The poem does not signify something beyond itself, no matter how ethereal, but aspires to produce and to dispose over the 'silence' that language alone creates.

In *Faux Pas*, it remained open to question whether the poetic claim to accomplish a fundamental disclosure should be taken as a reality, or merely as an illusion, a kind of artistic effect. In 'The Myth of Mallarmé', the question is decided in the negative. The realization towards which poetry is oriented – the freeing of the poem from the framework of representation and signification, its accomplishment in a work existing by itself, expressing silence – appears in the second part of the essay as an impossibility. The only means by which language can deliver us from the pressure of things – and, within language, from the reference to things – is through its 'thingly' nature: through its material properties, through 'sound, rhythm, number' (39, 31), or through the appearance of the written text (as in the typographical experiments of Mallarmé). The underlying intent of poetic language to free itself of natural reality, and to make present the absence at the origin of language, discovers itself in irreconcilable contradiction with its means. 'The contradiction is harsh, it tortures all poetic language, as it torments the speculations of Mallarmé' (45, 37).

III

'The Experience of Mallarmé' (*Nouvelle Revue Française* (NRF) 1952, collected in *L'Espace littéraire*,) introduces relatively little that is new in terms of the actual interpretation of Mallarmé. At this level, it consists primarily in a re-working of the arguments of 'The Myth of Mallarmé', translating these, as it were, into terms that resonate more closely with the somewhat different language and conceptuality of *L'Espace littéraire*. The questions that, in 'The Myth of Mallarmé', emerged from study of a relatively wide selection of texts, are here approached with great economy, through an interpretation of the radical separation between 'immediate' and 'essential language' (i.e. ordinary and literary language) announced in the 'Crise de vers': 'a brutal distinction, and yet one that is difficult to grasp', Blanchot writes (EL 38, 39).

The comment is worth reflecting upon, since the sense that there might be something 'difficult to grasp' about this distinction has not met with a sympathetic reception. Tzvetan Todorov, referring to this discussion of Mallarmé, sees in it 'Romantic commonplaces';

Stephen Schwarz writes that 'even in Mallarmé's time, this view of art was commonplace if not a downright cliché'; and Timothy Clark: 'Blanchot's account is thoroughly traditional in the vehemence with which it depends on maintaining a strict distinction between the aesthetic and the instrumental'.[12] Suspending for a moment the negative implications of these remarks, it certainly is important to recognize that the understanding of the poetic in terms of a strict separation from the language of the world goes well beyond Mallarmé. An influential study that makes this point and that collects a great deal of very relevant material by way of corroboration is Frank Kermode's *The Romantic Image*.[13] Kermode's historical thesis is that the desire to isolate poetic language from other kinds of discourse, for him centred in the idea of 'the image', is an essential tendency of modern literature and renders untenable the sharp opposition between Romantic and Modernist literature, fostered by writers such as T. E. Hulme and T.S. Eliot. Kermode's documentation of the continuity on this point is indeed so convincing that it can lead one to wonder if the 'Romantic image' is the best descriptive term for a characteristic that his own work shows to exceed the jurisdiction of such relatively narrow period and style concepts.

It remains, however, open to question whether the idea of the poetic that results should be considered as a purely historical phenomenon, something that we have now overcome and that we would interest ourselves with only in order to explain its historical determinants; or whether, on the other hand, there are elements in it by which it remains an unresolved part of our actuality. The decision cannot be merely a matter of an affirmation or negation in accordance with a given worldview, but depends on how one understands this idea of the poetic. This requirement tends to be obscured in the critical reception by the free use of labels such as formalism, aestheticism, 'art for art's sake', or the autotelic work. Each of these terms has its own provenance and its own theorists, but they all function in a similar way to anticipate the meaning of the phenomenon by the very term

---

12 Tzvetan Todorov, *Critique de la critique*, Paris: Editions du Seuil, 1984, 68; Stephen Schwarz, 'Faux Pas: Maurice Blanchot and the Ontology of Literature', *SubStance* 27/1(1998), 20; and Timothy Clark, 'Blanchot's Contradictory Passion: Inspiration in *The Space of Literature*', *SubStance* 25/1(1996),59.
13 *The Romantic Image*. London: Routledge, 1957.

that designates it, giving it a kind of self-evidence so that, far from attracting attention as something 'difficult to grasp', it appears to be already well understood. The depiction of modern poetics in Blanchot is entirely different: here, it is not a matter of producing poetry in the pure state, cleansed of all admixture of non-poetic elements, but of seeking to determine the sense of this possibility. This direction is evident in Mallarmé who, in 'Crise de vers', advances the 'magic concept of the Work' as an attempt at realizing what is tentatively expressed in the poetry of his contemporaries and the recent past.

In 'The Experience of Mallarmé', as in *La Part du feu*, the origins of Mallarmé's idea of the work are sought in the poet's reflections on language. This time, the analysis proceeds through a series of differentiations – between everyday language, the language of thought, the language of the autonomous poem, and finally, the work (*l'oeuvre*) (cf. EL 38–43, 39–42). These divisions, while aiming to clarify Mallarmé's thought, are worked out more or less independently by Blanchot, and form a detailed and step by step philosophical analysis of the essential possibilities of language. The text is rather rapid and compressed, but it communicates closely with other texts in *L'Espace littéraire*: in drawing out the thought, therefore, we will also gain a first view of the philosophical premises of this work.

The basic character of everyday language in this analysis is its instrumentality. We speak *with* and *through* language, in a movement projected towards the meaning that it serves to convey. In this movement, we necessarily overlook language itself, just as our work with tools does not focus on the tools themselves, but takes them for granted, and looks ahead towards the work that is to be completed.[14] In everyday use, language 'disappears marvellously at once, entirely, into its use' (39, 39). Since we overlook language, we tend also to overlook the work that it performs: we take it as giving us immediate access to the world, when in fact, it is 'charged with history' (40, 40). Hence the necessity for the critical analysis of the prejudices and valorizations that attach themselves to apparently neutral designations.

---

14 As is shown in Heidegger's description of the movement of withdrawal characteristic of equipment. cf. *Being and Time*, Section 15; and also Section 1 of 'The Origin of the Work of Art', now available in English in *Off the Beaten Track*. Trans. Julian Young and Kenneth Haynes. NY: Cambridge University Press, 2002.

This, however, is the role of 'the language of thought' (*la parole de la pensée*, 41, 41). Poetic language (*la parole poétique*, 42, 41) is given its sense in relation to a more fundamental, ontological reification. In naming, language posits a stability and an identity which is then assumed actually to exist. In language, entities 'take on the appearance of stable objects, existing one by one, and assume the certainty of the immutable' (40, 40). Everyday language tends to efface its own constitutive function, (*la parole a en elle le moment qui la dissimule*, 41, 40): it produces the impression of a world of discrete unitary objects, which are simply there to be named, and presents itself as merely one such object among others (namely, 'language').

For Blanchot, not only Mallarmé, but the modern thought of poetry more generally, is closely linked to a thinking of language. The observation seems at first entirely unsurprising: it seems evident that a clarification of the idea of language would be a natural preliminary step on the way to clarifying what is distinctive about literary language. But the question of poetry, as it is encountered in poetry itself, does not have the same sense as in a theoretical discourse, that would seek to define the properties of poetic (or literary) language, in contrast to other forms of language. Mallarmé's conception of poetry develops in connection with a *critical* attitude towards language as we ordinarily use and encounter it, a sense that everyday language is deceptive, and that the poetic activity offers the possibility of a language that is more 'true', that accomplishes itself in closer accord to what it is, as language.[15] In the text that we are reading, this idea is presented in ontological terms:

> In the language of the world, language is silent as the being of language and as the language of being, and by virtue of this silence, it is beings that speak: in this language, beings find the repose and assurance of things in the world. (41, 41)
>
> In poetic language, what is expressed is the fact that beings are silenced [. . .] Beings are silenced, but then being tends to

---

15 One finds an impressive confirmation of the wider literary–historical application of this thesis in Sanford Schwartz, *The Matrix of Modernism: Pound, Eliot and Early Twentieth-Century thought*. Princeton, NJ: Princeton UP, 1985. Schwartz shows a consistent suspicion of abstraction and habitual experience at work in modern poetics, and relates this suspicion to currents in the philosophical thought of the period, particularly Bergson.

come to language, and language wants to be. Poetic language is no longer the language of any speaker: in this language, no one speaks and that which speaks is not a person: rather it seems that language speaks itself. Language then takes on all its importance: it becomes the essential: language speaks as the essential and this is why the language of the poet can be called 'essential language'. (42, 41)

At this point, one notes, the explicit reference to Mallarmé has largely receded from view, the exposition having modulated in the course of a few pages into the philosophical terms proper to the critical text with little more than the bare schema of the 'brutal distinction' remaining from the source text. This kind of transition is indicative of the difficulties that *L'Espace littéraire* poses to its readers. The text itself does not provide clarification; like all the texts in *L'Espace littéraire*, 'The Experience of Mallarmé' proceeds in an extremely decisive fashion, but at no point pauses to explain or reflect upon its procedure.

Let us defer for the moment this question of the 'method', and confine ourselves to observing the critical argument as it is presented. After the passage cited, the text moves to distance itself from another conception with which Mallarmé is often associated. Blanchot remarks that the direction of the thought here – the poem as making visible its own language – evokes 'the familiar idea' of the poem as a 'universe of words whose relations, compositions, powers – through sound, figure and rhythmic mobility – are affirmed in a unified and sovereignly autonomous space' (42, 42). Rilke and Ponge are mentioned in passing, and it seems that these remarks are meant to apply to a wider historical tendency in poetics. Although the name does not actually come up, there is surely also a reference implied to Paul Valéry. In what is perhaps his most well-known essay on poetics, 'Poetry and Abstract Thought' (first published in 1939), Valéry describes language as divided between two essential axes, in terms very close to this text. The essay elaborates the division between the language of comprehension, which is used up in its employment, dissolved entirely in the transmission of meaning, and poetic language, in which the sensible characteristics, the tone, the voice acquire their own value, their own effectiveness. Poetic language constitutes a sphere which is in principle separate from the domain of everyday language, with its 'practical and statistical origin', in the same way that the world of musical sounds is separate from the continuous and inchoate production of noise.[16]

From a critical point of view, then, what is at stake in Blanchot's text is the possibility that the initiative of Mallarmé's poetics contains something more or other than is represented by this tendency within its reception and interpretation. As we have begun to see, the decisive difference is now formulated in terms of the relation between language and being. For Mallarmé, writes Blanchot, 'The work of art has its origin in being (*se reduit à l'être*). This is its task: to be, to make present "this word: it is . . . all the mystery is there"' (44, 43).[17] Although the vocabulary here marks a new departure, in comparison with the texts that we have been studying, the poetics that is now sketched out, on this basis, is recognizably related to the presentation in *La Part du feu*. In the pages that follow (EL 43–48, 43–46), the program for the complete realization of poetic language is recapitulated from the previous essay in passages of almost hallucinatory abstraction – in part condensing Poulet's study of Mallarmé, in *La Distance intérieure*.[18] In the poem, each word is absorbed into a perpetual movement of substitution and exchange, in which 'there are neither terms nor moments', only a 'pure agility of reflections, where nothing is reflected' (47, 45). But when it has 'suspended all possible beings' (that is to say, when it has dissolved all signification), the poem encounters its limit in 'this word, *it is*':

> a word which underlies all words, in letting itself be dissimulated by them, which when it is dissimulated, is their presence, their reserve, but, when they cease, presents itself [. . .], *moment de foudre, éclat fulgurant* . . . This moment is something like the work of the work, expressing the fact that the work is, apart from all signification, apart from any historical or aesthetic affirmation [. . .] (48, 45–46)

---

16 Paul Valéry, *Oeuvres*. Tome 1. Paris: Gallimard, 1957; see especially 1325–1326.
17 The passage refers to a remark in a letter of Mallarmé in which he identifies this aspiration as the centre of his projected and unfinished great work, 'the Book'. There are other passages which resonate with Heideggerean thought in Mallarmé's prose, especially the passage from the prose text, 'L'Action restreinte' on the impersonality of the work, discussed elsewhere in *L'Espace littéraire* (cf. 293–294, 222).
18 See especially Section IX of Poulet's study, which cites many of the passages that Blanchot uses. *La Distance intérieure*. Paris: Plon, 1952.

At the moment of its presence, when it 'is' apart from all signification, the work brings into the open 'the word being' – 'the word which underlies all words', their 'reserve', dissimulated in their ordinary usage but coming to light in the poem, as its 'work'. The conclusions are similar in their general direction to 'The Myth of Mallarmé', although the conceptuality is different. As in the earlier texts, Mallarmé's poetics is seen as oriented towards the integral realization of the poem. What is at stake in this enterprise is not a purification of the poetic quality, through the abstraction of all that is prosaic and referential, as is suggested in certain texts of Valéry. The poetic is not defined in terms of a particular property that can then be isolated and produced in the pure state, but in terms of the 'work' that the poem performs, in terms of what it allows to appear – the dissimulated presence or reserve of language, named, in the preceding text, as 'absence' or 'silence', and here, as 'the being of language' or 'this word, it is'.

IV

This text provides a convenient point of departure from which to approach one of the main difficulties of Blanchot's criticism. Reading Blanchot as a critic requires constant attention to the subtle shifts that occur, at times line by line, in the distance of the critical commentary and the degree of assent to the text under discussion. One has to become aware of this movement in reading 'The Experience of Mallarmé', where at a number of points the reference to Mallarmé seems to be little more than the occasion for a thought that unfolds in its own terms. Although there are variations of degree, some texts being more free and others more 'objective', this gesture is frequent in Blanchot: the work of criticism is at all points intimately bound up with a philosophical thought that at once informs the readings and finds in them the medium for its development. If it is not so marked in the text from *La Part du feu* that we studied here ('The Myth of Mallarmé'), it can be observed in a number of subsequent texts in the same collection.

'The Paradox of Aytré' can serve as an example. The essay is in part about a story by Jean Paulhan, but it also advances some very general claims about the ideal that animates literature as such:

> Literature claims to make language into an absolute, and to recognize this absolute as the equivalent of silence. If language

can become total, as poetry demands that it should [...], then it will need to transcend language, and, expressing itself at each moment as a totality, it will need at each moment to be entirely outside of language. Silence will then be attained through words, and it will be the sign of their accomplishment. (PF 69, 63)

A little later, Blanchot recalls that this is 'the myth of Mallarmé' – that is, that it corresponds to the conception of the 'Work' that Mallarmé evokes in his prose – but it is evident that this 'myth' is not considered primarily as the speculation of a particular poet; rather, Mallarmé's ideal gives expression to a demand proper to language, to realize itself integrally. In so doing, he makes visible a movement sketched out in all poetry: 'actual poetry is an effort towards this unrealizable aspiration, and (according to the poets) has its foundation in this impossibility and this contradiction, which it vainly seeks to realize' (PF 70, 64).

In *La Part du feu*, such claims are made almost incidentally, in texts that largely preserve the critical format; the impression created can be rather strange, since by their radicality, these statements seem to exceed the 'generic' purpose of the critical essay, its status as a contribution to the interpretation or the assessment of the particular author or work. In *L'Espace littéraire*, the conventions of the critical essay are less closely observed. A set of claims about language and literature link the various studies, creating a greater sense of a coherence and unity than in previous collections. In order to assess what this text presents at the level of interpretation – as in the reading of Mallarmé, which we have just been working through – one has to consider its relation to this discourse, developed in the course of the book as a whole.

One of the central axes of *L'Espace littéraire* is the notion of the work (*l'oeuvre*), the exposition of which occupies a number of the essays. Let us cite here the initial definitions of this theme, from the opening pages of *L'Espace littéraire*:

> The work – the work of art, the literary work – is neither finished nor unfinished: it is. What it says is exclusively this: that it is – and nothing more. (EL 14, 14)
>
> Whoever lives in the dependence of the work – be it to write it or to read it – belongs to the solitude of that which only expresses

the word being – the word that language shelters in dissimulating it or allows to appear in the silent void of the work. (15, 15)

One sees at once how close this is to the conception of the literary creation that is ascribed to Mallarmé in the text that we have just been reading: there, we recall, the task of the work of art is 'to be: to make present "this word: it is"' (EL 44, 43). We can see, too, that the relation of the commentary to Mallarmé's idea of the poem has been modified, in comparison with the texts that we have been examining from *La Part du feu*. In the earlier study, the exposition of the poetics is doubled by a critical discourse, which describes it as an unattainable ideal, shadowed by the consciousness of its impossibility.[19] Here, by contrast – if we can supply the conclusion to which the terms of the text itself unmistakably point – Mallarmé's poetics is seen as having discovered (or at least approximated) the truth of the work, proposed in Blanchot's own definitions. It is evident, then, that Mallarmé's work takes on its sense here within a horizon that is not derived from his text, and into which he has, at most, partial insight. Blanchot's idea of 'the work' – the work that says nothing more than that it *is* – functions then to make possible a critical perception, to see the demand that motivates Mallarmé's poetics, and to retrieve this understanding from the doctrines (such as aesthetic autonomy) into which it has subsequently precipitated and become known and familiar.

To locate the essence of the work of art in the fact that the work 'is' – and nothing more – is not to identify the artistic with the intensification of the materiality of the artistic medium (cf. EL 296, 223–224). That the work *is* – in an active and pronounced manner – signifies the revelation of being or, more precisely, the revelation of its concealment:

> In the world, being is negated, dissimulated (in this sense also protected): but in the work, on the other hand, in which dissimulation reigns, that which dissimulates itself tends to emerge in

---

19 In 'Literature and the Right to Death', when the claim of the poem to no longer represent, but simply to 'be' is recognized as a motivation in modern poetry, it is seen as a 'tragic effort', impossible to realize (PF 317, 328).

the depths of appearance, that which is negated becomes the excess of affirmation. (EL 320, 239)

'The world' here is the world of practical activity and effective communication, where words and things are absorbed in their use-value to the exclusion of their being. In the work, however 'that which is dissimulated (*ce qui se dissimule*) tends to emerge'. In its silent presence, its distance, its impersonality, the work is the appearance of the opacity of being in the midst of the intelligibility of the world.[20]

In order to understand this interpretation of the poetic, we have now to consider the structure of thought that it draws upon. The premises of Heideggerean thought seem to be simply assumed here as the element of the discourse. But this appropriation goes well beyond the appearance of the ontological difference in certain passages. The particular and unique character of *L'Espace littéraire*, as a treatment of the literary phenomenon, comes in part from the assimilation of the thought of being in the form that it takes in Heidegger. Perhaps no other work has to the same extent followed Heidegger in the leap across 'the abyss' separating thought from knowledge.[21] This transition is not always immediately visible in the detail of its literary–critical presentation, but it is only in these terms, I would suggest, that one can negotiate the extreme difficulty of situating Blanchot's work in relation to theory and criticism.

Through its immense and myriad explorations, Heidegger's thought avows itself always to be oriented by the question of being, its single and unique problem, from which all dimensions of existence are to be re-conceived, and all the philosophical writings of the past are to be re-read. The extent of this reflection is such that any claim to quickly render it would inevitably be facile, contrary to the formidable complexity of any of the main works, as well as to the ongoing work of reformulation that characterizes Heidegger's career.

---

20 As many texts make clear, this is not in any way to identify anything like the content or the meaning of works, or any aspect that would be simply present and verifiable. The work – '*n'ayant pas lieu en tant que d'aucun objet qui existe*' (Blanchot citing Mallarmé) – is only the experience of the work, only present for the reader and the writer who belong to it (see 'The Secret of the Golem', LV II.vii). We will return to this question of the conditions of the work later in our study, in Chapter 5.
21 cf. Heidegger, *Was heisst Denken?* Section 1.

Nonetheless, the primary focus of our study upon Blanchot demands a certain economy. Under these circumstances, our procedure will be to enter the terrain by way of one text, namely 'On the Essence of Truth' (in *Pathmarks*), an essay in which the thought of truth, which Heidegger had already developed in *Being and Time* and in his lectures of the 1920s, is recast in particularly concentrated form.[22]

The text undertakes to uncover the hidden foundations of the concept of truth at work in everyday life and in the discourse of scientific knowledge. For Heidegger, this form of truth can be circumscribed, grasped in its limits, by the recognition that it always and only concerns things of which it may be said that they *are*, and it does not and cannot touch upon the fact *that things are* in the first place. The claim to truth in the most ordinary sense – the correspondence of a statement or a representation to a reality – proceeds on the basis of the not fully explicated given that things are already discovered for us, and thus allow us to predicate truths of them. Our access to the evidence of things, such as they are, there *for us* – and not just in the indifferent mode of presence that Heidegger refers to as being present-at-hand (*Vorhandenheit*) – is here identified with a dimension of existence preceding and making possible the human as a power of speaking, knowing and acting. In the text with which we are concerned, this dimension is elaborated under the term 'freedom' ('On the Essence of Truth,' Section 4). Freedom here – in a special sense, expressly distinguished from received conceptions – designates the gesture of 'letting things be' (*das Seinlassen des Seienden*) – the prior movement by which, in interacting with things, we have always already 'allowed' things to show themselves, set them before us, let them lie there (*lassen sie liegen, lassen sie vor-liegen*). In Heidegger, this accomplishment is not a mediation of any kind: it is simply to give things over themselves, to

---

22 On this text, see Rodolphe Gasché, 'Tuned to Accord: On Heidegger's Concept of Truth' in *Of Minimal Things*, Stanford: Stanford UP, 1999; and John Sallis, 'Deformatives', in *Double Truth*, Albany, NY: SUNY Press, 1995. Among the German commentaries, particular mention should be given to Friedrich-Wilhelm von Herrmann who has devoted an entire book to the sentence by sentence analysis of Heidegger's essay, one that shows moreover that the text can well support such apparently excessive attention: *Wahrheit, Freiheit, Geschichte*, Frankfurt a.M.: Klostermann, 1992.

allow them to be what they are. The 1928 lecture course *Einleitung zur Philosophie* develops the conception with particular clarity:

> This letting things be in the widest sense is situated fundamentally prior to every particular interest or determinate indifference. Our letting-be, our giving things over to themselves and to their being, is an indifference that belongs to the metaphysical essence of the *Dasein*. This 'indifference' is only possible in care [. . .] To let beings be is not at all nothing. Certainly, we do not actually do anything, in order that, for example, nature is what and how it is; we add nothing, and yet this letting-be is an 'act' of the highest and most original kind, possible only on the basis of the innermost essence of our existence, freedom.[23]

The initial possibility of a relation to beings is a moment of 'indifference', a passivity at the core of our concern for our own being, of the 'care' (*Sorge*) that defines human existence (*Dasein*). This moment of 'indifference' signifies that we are 'free' for things in the sense that we allow ourselves to encounter them, that we let them be what they are. But this neutral presence to things has its own ground in a still deeper dimension of 'freedom':

> To let be – that is, to let beings be as the entities that they are – means to engage oneself with the open region and its openness, into which every being comes to stand, bringing that openness, as it were, along with itself. Western thinking in its beginning conceived this region as *ta aletheia*, the unconcealed [. . .] [F]reedom is engagement in the disclosure of beings as such. Disclosedness itself is conserved in ek-sistent engagement, through which the openness of the open, that is, 'the there' [*das Da*] – is what it is (*Pathmarks*, 144–145).[24]

---

23 *Einleitung zur Philosophie*, vol. 27 of the *Gesamtausgabe*. Frankfurt: Klostermann, 2001, 102–103.
24 Passages from 'On the Essence of Truth' are cited following the translation of John Sallis in the English translation of Heidegger's *Wegmarken* collection: *Pathmarks*. Ed. William McNeil. Cambridge: Cambridge UP, 1998.

The open is the 'space', the dimension within which things as such can show themselves, can be evident (*offenbar*).²⁵ If it belongs to the human manner of being that it allows beings to be, this is because in advance of all interaction with that which is, it has let itself into the open. Hence it can, as it were, bring this open to entities, allowing them to show themselves, and thus to *be*.

In the subsequent section of the text, the relation to the open is located in the mood or attunement (*Stimmung*), permeating all activity. Through this attunement, all our activity is sustained in the evidence of the open. But while we have a non-thematic understanding of being in 'mood', we are turned away from it by consciousness and activity. Existence is structured by an openness to beings, but it is also engaged in a work of concealment. 'Letting-be is intrinsically at the same time a concealing' (*Pathmarks*, 148). In entering into the open and taking possession in language of what is disclosed therein, we allow the open itself to withdraw. The openness to things is accomplished by a turning away from the openness (or evidence, *Offenbarkeit*) of beings as such: this turning away is here referred to as the 'concealment of beings as a whole':

> The concealment of beings as a whole, un-truth proper, is older than every openedness of this or that being. It is older even than the letting-be itself, which in disclosing already holds concealed, and comports itself to concealing. What conserves letting-be in this relatedness to concealing? Nothing less than the concealing of what is concealed as a whole, of beings as such, that is, the mystery; not a particular mystery regarding this or that, but rather the one mystery – that in general, mystery (the concealing of what is concealed) as such holds sway throughout the *Da-sein* of human beings. (*Pathmarks*, 148)

---

25 This space is not physical space; rather, it is in the open that the phenomenon of spatiality – that is the articulation of differences such as here and there, near and far, as opposed to the indifferent space of geometry or physics – first becomes possible; cf. 'Letter on Humanism': 'being is the "dimension" of existence as ek-static. The dimension is not however space in the sense that we know it. Rather all spatiality and all time-space is within the dimension, being itself' (*Pathmarks*,142–143; *Wegmarken*, 337).

Despite the superficial resemblance, this is not conceived along the lines of optical phenomena – that in focussing on a particular thing, for example, we lose the sense of the whole, or even that in seeing light, we must also necessarily see darkness. It is not a matter of the limit or the background of language and knowledge here, but its origin, *der ständige Herkunft aller Lichtung*, the constant origin of all clearing (*Holzwege*, 41): hence this concealing (*die Verbergung des Verborgene*) is 'the un-truth' that is the essence of truth.[26]

This brief sketch of 'On the Essence of Truth' can allow us to locate some of the conceptual coordinates of the presentation of the work of art in *L'Espace littéraire*. At intervals throughout this work, Blanchot states, with the force of an axiom, that the work of art or the poem is the site at which being comes to appearance: in the language of the poem 'being tends to come to language, and language wants to be' (EL 42, 41); in the work of art 'that which dissimulates itself tends to emerge in the depths of appearance' (EL 320, 239). Heidegger's text has been reviewed here in order to sketch out the thought that is contained in these affirmations. In everyday language and in our experience in the world, we relate 'immediately' to things, which we assume to be simply present to our powers of knowledge and transformation. Through the reflection on the question of being, Heidegger claims to discover a dimension of language and existence that is prior to ('older than') this active relation to things in the world, prior even to the consciousness of self. In speaking of things, and even in practically dealing with them, we have to do with things that 'are', and this implies that we have first allowed them to *be*, and that in advance of all encounter with things, we have engaged and discovered ourselves in 'the open' (the unconcealment of beings). As the condition of our access to the world, being continues to prevail over all our relations. In the familiarity of our habitual relations to the world, the relation to being is reserved in concealment: but the sheltering and the retreat of being is not an inviolable law. The determination of the initial entry into the open as 'freedom' implies that the human has the possibility of renewing

---

26 As Heidegger writes in the essay on the Anaximander fragment: '*Die Unverborgenheit des Seienden, die ihm gewährte Helle, verdunkelt das Licht des Seins. Das Sein entzieht sich indem es sich in das Seiende entbirgt [. . .] Das Sichversehen des Menschen entspricht dem Sichverbergen der Lichtung des Seins. [. . .] Indem [die A-letheia] Unverborgenheit des Seienden bringt, stiftet sie erst Verborgenheit des Seins*' (*Holzwege*, 337).

the encounter with being, and thereby also gaining a renewed access to the open of the world.

Our primary concern here is with how this thought functions in relation to the work of a critical understanding. The genetic perspective that is created by studying the sequence of essays on Mallarmé allows one to see the Heideggerean language of this presentation in relation to the ongoing critical concerns of Blanchot's work. The comparison tends to suggest that this intervention is not really a fundamental transformation in the direction of the interpretation. Rather, it appears as a further step in the clarification of a position whose basic tendency is consistent from the earliest texts onwards. The rigour and the immanence demanded by poetry, in Mallarmé's conception, is at all points conceived in terms of its original function as a mode of language, which is to give language the reality and presence that it lacks when it functions as an instrument of communication and understanding: 'what [Mallarmé] wants is to give language existence (*de faire exister la parole*) [. . .]' (PF 39, 39). This intention should not be assimilated to a very widespread conception of modern poetry, for which it is distinguished by a more acute consciousness of language, in its materiality, its productive indetermination, and its power to mediate or even create experience. What is understood by 'language' (*le langage*, *la parole*) in the context of this reflection is something entirely different than the object of philology, linguistics and semantics. In 'The Myth of Mallarmé', the poetic structuring of the material properties of language, the movement of 'transposition' that attenuates meaning, is oriented towards realizing the absence that is the possibility of language: the intention of the poem is to make present the 'mysterious silence, the obscure ground against which everything makes itself present' (PF 45, 38). In considering such statements, one sees that the apparent shift marked by the Heideggerean language introduced in *L'Espace littéraire* is not in fact so very great. What is approached under 'absence' in *La Part du feu*, we can now see, is nothing other than the question of being: 'absence', like the open in Heidegger, is a means of naming and thinking the 'space', the element in which things are given with language. Such an angle of approach would by no means be excluded within the terms of Heideggerean thought, for which it is axiomatic that the 'same' can be thought under an entirely different conceptual language;

Heidegger's readings of poetic works as engaged in the interpretation of being depend on this premise.[27] At this point, we can begin to see the crux that is revealed for literary criticism by Blanchot's work. The essential deciding factor in this interpretation of Mallarmé and of modern poetry is not a matter of exegesis, of textual understanding, but of the horizon of presuppositions within which the results of exegesis take on their sense. Literary criticism, regardless of whether we take this to include wider social and cultural processes of reception or limit it to the disciplinary field of knowledge and research, cannot simply accept or dispute in its own terms the claim that the poem in Mallarmé is oriented toward making present language as a power of absence and contestation. Before any exegetic discussion of this claim can get underway, the critical discourse would have to clarify its own relation to 'absence' or to 'being' – that is, what its own language implies about the fact that things 'are' for us. In a reading of Mallarmé that sees his thought as a prescient expression of modern linguistic self-consciousness, the horizon of the meaning of the poem converges without apparent rupture with the theory of textuality that is also available in discursive form. Terms such as 'absence' or 'being', however, do not refer to real entities within the conceptual horizon that informs literary criticism. We have encountered the same problem (in Chapter 2) in the reading of Hölderlin, with the use of the term 'the sacred'. In dealing with modern poetry, literary criticism encounters a thought and a language with which it does not have continuity of assumptions. The decision on how this discontinuity is negotiated is bound to be largely determining for the resultant critical understanding. Perhaps the most common solution is to group such moments under the term 'metaphysics' (often used in a very inclusive sense) or to draw comparisons with theological thought. M. H. Abrams, for example, in the context of a discussion of Mallarmé, writes that 'modern claims about the nature and superlative value of the autonomous work of art owe both their form and their persuasive force not to an aesthetic, but to a theological prototype'.[28] Theology and metaphysics can provide a set of identifiable analogues through which the discontinuity between

---

27 For a statement to this effect, see Heidegger's essay 'Dichterisch wohnt der Mensch', *Vorträge und Aufsätze*. Pfullingen: Günther Neske, 1954, 187.
28 'Coleridge, Baudelaire and Modern Poetics', in *The Correspondent Breeze: Essays on English Romanticism*. New York: Norton, 1984, 134. A similar point of view is

poetry and the critic can be mediated. Although not usually part of the critical discourse itself, such ideas exist within a determinable relation to its own implicit or explicit methodology. If this path is taken, it is almost inevitable that the critical analysis becomes diagnostic and corrective. Religious or metaphysical tendencies in poetry and poetics become a compensatory reaction to the historical waning of religious belief, to the Kantian restrictions on philosophical speculation, to the rise of scientific positivism or to a materialistic and utilitarian culture. Such an understanding does not absolutely rule out any kind of positive assessment: one can admire the linguistic effects that can be derived from the imaginative adoption of an intrinsically unsustainable system of beliefs, even assent to it as a protest against the rationalism of modern ideology, but the assumptions of the poets are not then granted any credence in themselves, and only have validity within the confines of an identifiable literary movement.

To describe the basic critical effect of works such as *La Part du feu* and *L'Espace littéraire*, one could say, by contrast, that they represent a claim for the legitimacy of modern poetry. The certainty of the significance of the transformation represented by Mallarmé informs all of the essays that have been studied here, and makes up part of what is so distinctive about them. The critical stance of *L'Espace littéraire*, as we have seen by the example of Mallarmé, has the structure of an explication of a discovery. This stance, which has to some extent to be drawn out from the text, is stated more starkly in later works. With Mallarmé, Blanchot writes in 'L'Absence de livre', the final text of *L'Entretien infini,* 'writing opens on to writing' (EI 620, 422), and in the preface, again in reference to Mallarmé, he speaks of writing having slowly freed its own force, and thus opened a series of philosophical questions to which this work is dedicated (EI vii, xii). The idea of literature that emerges with Mallarmé (again, considered as an index, not as a progenitor) is not here something that belongs to the past, the characteristic of a period or a movement that can now be the object of a retrospective historical understanding: it is seen as an event that still remains to be thought, and that has a claim upon the present historical moment: hence, the advent of modern literature can appear as the announcement of a turning point that is still before us.

---

argued in Jean-Marie Schaeffer, *The Art of the Modern Age.* Trans. Steven Randall. Princeton, NJ: Princeton UP, 2000.

4 The Ambiguity of the Negative

I

Throughout Blanchot's critical essays, and above all, in the essays devoted to key figures such as Mallarmé, Kafka and Hölderlin, the direction that art and literature takes in the modern age is studied in the closest connection with an unfolding philosophical thought. The first significantly developed treatment of this thought appears in the texts of *La Part du feu* (1949, collecting texts written from 1945 onwards). The language of these texts shows the extent to which Blanchot's work is informed by the French philosophical environment of the time. In particular, it shows the influence of the interpretation of Hegel by Kojève – an influence circulating in many French thinkers, including Bataille, Sartre, Lacan and others, creating a common set of topics and a common conceptual language that links otherwise divergent projects.[1] In Blanchot, the philosophical questions generated within this environment are most often treated in the context of studies of literary writers and literary topics. In *La Part du feu*, for example, a sequence of essays ('The Myth of Mallarmé,' 'The Mystery in Letters', 'The Paradox of Aytré') draw upon and develop the ideas of Mallarmé in order to sketch out a theory of language. In the course of this exposition, the question of the structure of language opens on to a more general reflection on existence as conditioned by language. The primary accomplishment of language is identified with

---

1 On Blanchot and Hegel/Kojève see Marlene Zarader: *L'Être et le neutre*. Paris: Verdier, 2001, 41–59; and Anne-Lise Schulte Nordholt, *Maurice Blanchot: l'écriture comme experience du dehors*. Geneva: Droz, 1995, Chapter 2, entitled 'Le Langage, la négation, la mort'. On the history of the Hegelian movement in French thought, see Vincent Descombes, *Modern French Philosophy*. Trans. L. Scott-Fox and J.M. Harding. Cambridge UP, 1980; Judith Butler, *Subjects of Desire: Hegelian Reflections in Twentieth-Century France*. NY: Columbia UP, 1987; and Michael Roth, *Knowing and History: Appropriations of Hegel in Twentieth-Century France*. Ithaca: Cornell UP, 1988.

the possibility of being present to things from a distance: only on this basis are we able to manipulate and modify things, by placing them into new possible relations. In speaking and knowing, in relating to things in language, the human comes to occupy and move ever more in an element constituted by the tendential absence of all immediate reality. Language is the power to 'create empty space around us, to put a distance between ourselves and things' (PF 46, 39).

Despite the fact that it shows little inclination for synthesis or recapitulation, Blanchot's work is characterized by a high degree of continuity. The thought tends to develop through repetition and restatement, rather than by a linear sequential progression, and constantly returns to the same basic insights from different angles. I will study three texts here, each of which represents a significant step in the unfolding of a philosophical thought that is pursued throughout his writings. This sequence is considered, however, with a view to an understanding of Blanchot's literary criticism: it will allow us to move beyond the affinities and parallels between certain literary figures and twentieth-century philosophical discourse that appear in Blanchot's work, and see how the philosophical thought creates the horizon of the critical studies, imposing a decision that conditions the direction of the readings from the beginning.

The first of the texts to be examined is 'Literature and the Right to Death,' the long concluding essay of *La Part du feu*. The concern here will not be to provide a synthetic explication of the essay as such, but rather to draw upon those passages which allow the most direct approach to Blanchot's philosophical thought.[2] This text was first published over two issues of *Critique*, in 1947–1948. In its book publication, the division of the essay into two relatively autonomous parts is entirely effaced, as part of what seems like a deliberate elimination of organizing articulations. I begin with a passage

---

2   On 'Literature and the Right to Death' see Rodolphe Gasché, 'The Felicities of Paradox', in *Of Minimal Things: Studies in the Notion of Relation*. Stanford: Stanford UP, 1999; Christopher Fynsk, 'Crossing the Threshhold: On "Literature and the Right to Death"', in *Language and Relation: ... that there is language*. Stanford: Stanford UP, 1996; and James Swenson, 'Revolutionary Sentences', in *Yale French Studies*, vol. 93, 1998, 11–28.

from the beginning of what was, in its first appearance, the second part of the essay:

> Hölderlin, Mallarmé and in general, all those whose poetry has the essence of poetry as its theme, have seen a disquieting marvel in the act of naming. The word gives me what it signifies, but first it suppresses it. In order that I can say, this woman, it is necessary in one way or another that I deprive her of her reality of flesh and bone, make her absent, annihilate her. The word gives me the being, but it gives it to me deprived of being. The word is the absence of this being, its nothingness, that which remains of it when it has lost its being; the pure fact that it is not. From this point of view, language is a strange right. In a text anterior to the *Phenomenology*, Hegel, close here to his friend Hölderlin, wrote that: "the first act, by which Adam made himself master of the animals, was to impose a name upon them; that is, he annihilated them in their existence (as existents)."[3] By this, Hegel means that from this instant, the cat ceases to be a cat which is only real, and becomes an idea as well. The meaning of speech demands then, as the preface to all speech, a kind of immense hecatomb, a prior deluge, plunging all of creation into the sea. God had created beings, but man had to destroy them. It was only then that they assumed a meaning for man, and that he created them in his turn, on the basis of this death into which they had disappeared; however, in place of beings, and, as one says, of existents, there was now only being, and man was condemned not to be able to approach or live anything, except by way of the meaning which he is obliged to give to it. He discovered himself enclosed in the light, and he knew that the light could not finish, because the end itself was light, because it was from the end of beings that their signification (which is being)

---

3 In 'The Great Refusal' (an essay in *L'Entretien infini* which resumes some of the themes of 'Literature and the Right to Death') Blanchot speaks of a 'sacrifice' implicit in language as central to Hölderlin's thought, developing the idea through an intensive exegesis of a few lines from the poem 'Wie wenn am Feiertage' (EI 51–52, 39–40). The reference to Hölderlin in the passage cited here alludes to the early philosophical text, 'Urteil und Sein', which posits an initial division (*Ur-teil*) at the origin of thought and language, articulating a previous, more unified order (called 'being', *Sein*).

had come. (*Il se vit enfermé dans le jour, et il sut que ce jour ne pouvait pas finir, car la fin elle-même était lumière, puisque c'est de la fin des êtres qu'était venue leur signification, qui est l'être*). (PF 312–313, 322–323)

The text characteristically begins with an observation about certain writers – specifically about those of whom it can be said that their poetry 'has the essence of poetry as its theme'. It contains a claim on the purely critical level – that such poets share a marked concern with language and here, with the act of naming. But the text moves on to develop this question in its own terms, drawing, not on these poets, but on the conception of language as negation in Hegel, above all here, in the Jena lectures. The transition points to the close intertwining of literary criticism and philosophical thought in Blanchot.

At first sight, the use of Hegel seems to propose that the formation of the name (or the concept) can be understood in terms of the structure of dialectical overcoming (*Aufhebung*) in Hegel. The word would be the 'overcoming' of the thing, its annihilation as an individual, physical reality (its 'existence' in Blanchot's text) and its conservation at a higher level of ideality, that of the signification (also termed 'being' in this passage). But there are signs that this is not the whole picture. At the end of the passage we have cited, there is a suggestion – although it is not fully explained at this point – that, in giving us access to the dimension of the concept, language excludes us from a more immediate relation to things. This suffices in itself to indicate the limits of the appropriation of Hegel, since it runs contrary to a central tenet of his work, expressed in the *Phenomenology of Spirit* – in the critique of Kantian epistemology at the beginning of the 'Introduction' to this work, and, in another way, in the chapter on 'Sense-Certainty' – that universality is the irreducible element of thought, and that, as such, it cannot be understood as a reductive abstraction derived from a more original immediacy.

To think language in terms of negativity requires some modifications in the conception of negation presented by Kojève's explications, where the concern is with work, conflict and history. It is only to a certain degree that language can be assimilated to the more general category of transformative work. One can say that to name and to conceptualize is to overcome the opacity of things in their natural or immediate state, to acquire them as ideal being. Taken as a total phenomenon, however, language cannot be understood as a gradual and progressive negation like that by which natural and social givens are confronted and successively overcome, since it has first to appear 'all at once', so to speak. This is indicated in the passage above, when language is said to suppose the 'global' negation (or sacrifice, the 'hecatomb') of all that is:

> The meaning of speech demands then, as the preface to all speech, a kind of immense hecatomb, a prior deluge, plunging all of creation into the sea [. . .] In place of beings, and, as one says, of existents, there was now only being, and man was condemned not to be able to approach or live anything, except by way of the meaning which he is obliged to give to it. (313–314, 323)

In order to approach this point, I would like to suggest, one has to see how the conceptual language of Hegel (and his French reception) is here opened to Heideggerean thought. At first sight, certainly, the passages we have been citing seem remote from Heidegger's problematic, especially with respect to their deployment of the term 'being'. In Blanchot's sketch, the advent of language and world entails that there can no longer be any 'beings' or 'existents'; rather, there is only 'being' – a word which is here glossed as the 'meaning' which we give to beings (*le sens qu'il lui fallait faire naître*) or, later in the text, as 'logical and expressible truth' (*Il y a l'être, c'est à dire une vérité logique et exprimable* [. . .], 324, 336). In encountering things through the medium of language, Blanchot writes, the 'existent' – the thing in its presence – is called out of 'the obscure, cadaverous reality of its original reserve, and is only given the life of the spirit in exchange' (PF 316, 326). 'Being' here, then, is the space of a light which we shed over all creation, by which it becomes intelligible, but through which a more original 'existence', prior to logic and meaning, is excluded. This is certainly tending in a different direction to the thought of the ontological difference in Heidegger. In Heidegger's terms, one could say that the only way in which we could conceive of an original, pre-human reality, would be *by way of* the understanding of being. Nor does the understanding of things in their being necessarily give a 'signification' to things, much less make them logical and intelligible; of that which is illogical and meaningless, one says, nonetheless, that it 'is'.⁴ The passage is not at all, then, Heideggerean in a narrow sense. That said, however, the decisive premise for the orientation of the thought, the concern with the initial occupation of the space of light (*le jour*), within which the human way of relating to things becomes possible, brings Blanchot's thought closer to the questions which are addressed by Heidegger, and separates it to some extent from French philosophers of the period, such as Kojève, Sartre or even Bataille, who take their theoretical orientation from an immanent critique of Hegelian dialectic.

Let us turn, then, to Heidegger, in order to get a better sense of the common ground, and thus to prepare the way for an approach to the specificity of Blanchot's thought. In 'On the Essence of Truth' (as we have seen in our preceding chapter), Heidegger proposes that the openness of the human (*Dasein*) – that is to say, the fact that it is part of our existence that we are alongside beings, that whenever we are, we also discover beings, allow them to show themselves – has its foundation in the more original relation, by which we engage ourselves in the 'open' (*das Offene*).⁵ This text presents a compressed and schematized version of a problematic that is repeatedly recast in the texts written by Heidegger in the period after *Being and Time*. In order to demonstrate the affinity with Blanchot's thought, I would like here to examine another, earlier text – the treatise 'On the Essence of Ground' ('*Vom Wesen des Grundes*'), written in 1928. Heidegger's texts constantly reconsider the basic relations implied by the question of being from different angles, and by way of different terminologies, and there is much to be gained for grasping the contours of any given development by examining some of its anticipations and repetitions. 'On the Essence of Ground' has an historical interest in this context, since it is one of the first translations to be published in France.⁶ The

---

4   My remarks here draw on Derrida's discussion of the distortion of Heidegger by Levinas in 'Violence and Metaphysics', in *L'Écriture et la différence*. Paris: Editions du Seuil, 1967, 117–228.
5   Cf. our Chapter 3. There is a brief text by Blanchot from 1950, entitled 'Hölderlin', that centres on the figure of 'the open' in Hölderlin and Heidegger: *La Condition Critique: Articles 1945–1998*. Ed. Christophe Bident. Paris: Gallimard, 2010, 181–183.
6   The reception of Heidegger in France is studied in Dominique Janicaud, *Heidegger en France*, two vols. Paris: Albin Michel, 2001.

affinities to Heideggerean thought in *La Part du feu* seem to me to point more to this work, which is closer in its style to the fundamental ontological horizon of *Being and Time* than to Heidegger's works of the 1930s and 1940s.

The discussion will be confined to a brief diagonal through this formidable treatise, the aim being merely to locate certain of Blanchot's premises within the far more technical and step-by-step construction of Heidegger's treatise. The first section of 'On the Essence of Ground' traces the same path which we have already followed in 'On the Essence of Truth,' seeking to discover the foundations of the truth of knowledge and representation in existence and the relation to being. In the first place, propositional truth is said to be dependent on an initial discoveredness of things, here termed 'ontic truth'. Ontic truth, Heidegger states, is given first in pre-predicative experience, that is to say, in volitional and affective existence.[7] But this kind of evidence is grounded in what Heidegger calls 'ontological truth': this term here signifies the prior disclosedness of being, which first makes possible the discoveredness of all that is (*Enthülltheit des Seins ermöglicht erst Offenbarkeit des Seienden*, *Wegmarken*, 131, cf. *Pathmarks* 103–104). For Heidegger, any kind of relation to things that are – any kind of making or knowing, for example – including the relation to the self, is guided and lighted in advance by a prior understanding of being. This understanding is not a formal conception or in any way explicitly philosophical. It is formed in advance of the emergence of the particular self, in what Heidegger calls the transcendence of *Dasein* (cf. *Pathmarks* 107–108). As *Dasein*, the human is defined by an initial 'transcendence' of all beings, of everything that is. Hence it is that the human cannot be thought of as merely one being in the midst of the whole of beings. No doubt it is *also* one of the many beings, in this sense, but it is distinguished in that it has an anticipatory grasp of the *wholeness* of what is (121–123). This sense of the wholeness (*die Ganzheit*) of what is – the world in *Being and Time* – does not belong

---

7 '*Das ontische Offenbaren selbst aber geschieht im stimmungsmassig und triebhaft Sichbefinden inmitten von Seienden und in den hierin mitgegründeten strebensmässigen und willentlichen Verhaltungen zum Seienden*' Wegmarken. Frankfurt: Klostermann, 131. When not citing the original of this text, I will refer to the English translation: *Pathmarks*. Ed. William McNeil. Cambridge: Cambridge UP, 1998.

within the sphere of ontic truth, as one possible object for understanding. The phenomenon of world has been 'passed over' in the tradition of ontology, as Heidegger argues in *Being and Time*, because of the inadequacy of received categories to grasp it: 'world' is not an object for the subject, it is not even something that is (*ein Seiendes*). Rather, it is the ground, 'the first from out of which' on which all relations to beings are founded (98–99). The prior understanding of being (the prior projection of being, *Entwurf von Sein*) is given in the projection of the world, from which we come back to understand specific things in the world (cf. 122–123).

This sense of the relation to being, as a prior elevation over all particular relations, is the decisive point which, it seems to me, allows for the comparison to the explications of 'Literature and the Right to Death'. One can readily transpose Blanchot's arguments into the terms of the more developed conceptual apparatus of Heidegger. 'Ontic truth' becomes in Blanchot the givenness of things in language, that is to say, in the element of absence constituted by language. Let us recall the key propositions of the passage from 'Literature and the Right to Death':

> The word gives me the being, but it gives it to me deprived of being. It is the absence of this being, its nothingness, that which remains of it when it has lost its being, that is to say, purely the fact that it is not. (PF 312, 322)

As, in Heidegger, ontic truth is grounded in ontological truth, so, in Blanchot, our access to entities in their absence is grounded in a relation to absence *as such*, to nothingness 'in itself'. Absence or nothingness would then be 'ontological truth' in Blanchot, that which must be disclosed or given to us in some way, in order that we can relate to 'absents', to things in their absence – in order, that is, that we can speak of them.

This tendency of the argument is already visible in the essays on Mallarmé, in which the analysis moves from language as a 'power of absence and contestation' to its condition and possibility in 'silence', as the 'obscure ground upon which all things show themselves' (*fond obscur sur lequel tout se déclare*) (PF 45, 38). The same movement is present in the continuation of these reflections of 'Literature and the

Right to Death.' Here this initial absence is equated with the presence of death in the world:

> No doubt my language does not kill anyone. However, when I say 'this woman', her real death is announced and already present in my language; my language means that this person who is present, now, can be separated from herself, subtracted from her existence and her presence, and suddenly plunged into a void of existence and presence; my language essentially signifies the possibility of this destruction; at every moment, it is a resolute allusion to such an event.[8] [. . .] It is hence precisely correct to say: when I speak, death speaks in me. My language is the announcement that death is, at this very moment, loose in the world, that it has brusquely arisen between I who speak and the person I address: it is between us, as the distance that separates us, but this distance is also what prevents us from being separated, for in it is located the condition of all possible understanding.[9] Only death allows me to grasp what I want to attain: it is, in words, the sole possibility of meaning. Without death, everything would collapse into the absurd, into nothingness. (313, 323–324)

In speaking, then, what I first relate to is not the thing that is present; what is designated by my language is not a present entity. The act of naming is mediated by the future absence or death of the thing, which it traverses on the way to language. This also means that the practical and cognitive use of language as an instrument cannot be taken as the primary phenomenon, as the model for interpreting the being of language. For one cannot simply see the self (the human) as the one distinguished by the capability of suspending reality, of voiding things in order to manipulate them as words and images. On the contrary, the self also relates to itself through language, if

---

8 The form of this deduction in the passage cited draws on a passage of Kojève; cf. *Introduction à la lecture de Hegel*. Paris: Gallimard, 1947, 372–375.
9 'On the Essence of Ground' concludes with the statement that 'the human being [...] is a creature of distance. Only through originary distances that he forms for himself in his transcendence with respect to all beings does a true nearness to things begin to arise in him.' (*Pathmarks* 135).

in no other way, at least through the word 'I', and as such, it is subject to the same condition as anything that is given in the domain of 'meaning':

> When I speak, I negate the existence of what I say, but I also negate the existence of the one who speaks: my language, when it reveals being in its non-existence, affirms that this revelation is based in the non-existence of the one who reveals, in his power to separate from himself, to be other than his being. [. . .] Language only begins with the void: no presence, no certainty speaks; something essential is lacking from the one who expresses himself. Negation is bound to language. At the point of departure, I do not speak in order to say something, it is rather a nothing that demands to speak: nothing speaks, nothing finds its being in language, and the being of language is nothing. (313–314, 324)

Such formulations produce, to a pronounced degree, the impression of 'negativity' – in the ordinary rather than in the Hegelian sense – which must strike any reader on first encountering Blanchot, and which has undoubtedly had a discouraging effect upon the reception of his work. It is important, then, to see that this is not primarily a matter of a 'dark' vision of things, but rather of a conceptual language that is employed to approach questions which, taken in themselves, do not directly entail either an optimistic or a pessimistic assessment of human existence. The comparison with Heidegger indicates that Blanchot's language is guided by a philosophical problematic that can be also be explored by different paths, and in a different language, as is evident from the striking contrast between the style of Heidegger and Blanchot's texts. The surface contrast has obscured the real proximity of the thought: by a not too abusive reduction, one could say that Blanchot, when not denounced as nihilistic, has often been praised for 'going beyond' Heidegger in being more negative in his language and conclusions. Once one begins to see the degree of common ground in the orientation of Blanchot and Heidegger, then this apparent 'negativity' can cease to exercise its undue domination over the reception of Blanchot.

The common philosophical ground has been summed up by Foucault, in his important article on Blanchot, when he speaks of a convergence within contemporary philosophy around the separation of the being of language from subjectivity.[10] This formula can be glossed in terms of the present discussion by saying that, in 'Literature and the Right to Death', the original phenomenon of language is detached from the self, speaking out of itself, as present, designating knowledge of or feelings about present things. In distancing this 'natural' view of language, Blanchot's standpoint, we have been suggesting, is essentially similar to that formulated in the Heideggerean thesis that, prior to any selfhood or positive determination of body or mind, language, world and self are constituted by an initial transcendence of all that is. In Blanchot, the totality (*Ganzheit*) within which things are given is the element of the 'light' (*le jour*). In the 'light' of language, things lose their existence and receive in exchange the 'life of the spirit' (meaning, or, in the terms of the text, 'being'). Blanchot can say 'death speaks' or 'nothing finds its being in language' because our occupation of the 'light' – the world of meaning – cannot be derived solely out of ourselves, as a cognitive and volitional unity. Rather, as in Heidegger, the human, the speaking being, first stands outside of itself, in relation to the 'first absence upon which emerge all our gestures, all our acts and the very possibility of our words [. . .]' (PF 77, 72). All our relations to things are guided and lit in advance by the prior 'understanding' of this nothingness, an understanding that we necessarily have from the moment at which we enter the space within which we can name and know things (i.e. the space of the 'light', *le jour, l'être*).

This said, however, there remains an element in Blanchot which is not less difficult to recognize in terms of the Heideggerean analogy than in Hegelian terms – the sense that the opening of language and world is at the same time an enclosure, that man is 'condemned not to be able to approach or live anything, except by way of the meaning which he is obliged to give to it'. There is no such a 'condemnation' of existence in Heidegger. Even aside from the non-conformism with respect to Heidegger – whose work has, after all, only been proposed here as an analogy for understanding – this claim is a difficult aspect of Blanchot's argument. On the one hand, Blanchot proposes something like a transcendental analysis, describing the structure and the possibility of the conceptual disposal over things taken for granted in

---

10 'Maurice Blanchot, the Thought from Outside', trans. Brian Massumi, in *Foucault/Blanchot*. New York: Zone, 1987, 7–60.

the ordinary course of our existence; on the other hand, he uncovers an inadequacy within this disposal, declaring it void of content. There comes to seem an almost gnostic tendency in his thought; it is as if the very condition which enables us to have a relation to things already rendered them empty and worthless.[11]

This tendency of the argument remains indeed often very difficult to grasp at a number of the points at which it surfaces in *La Part du feu*. But if we turn now to the concluding passages of 'Literature and the Right to Death', where, after many twists and turns, the essay enters into its concluding exposition, we can begin to grasp the coherence of the thought. Here, Blanchot begins to suggest that language and meaning are marked with a fundamental ambiguity as a result of a certain unreliability affecting our power of negation:

> There is being – that is, a logical and expressible truth – and there is a world because we can destroy things and suspend existence. This is the sense in which one can say that there is being because there is nothingness: death is the possibility of man, his chance, it is through death that there remains for us the future of a world finding its accomplishment: death is the greatest hope for men, the sole hope of being men. This is why existence is their sole true anxiety, as Levinas has shown. Existence is frightening, not because of the death that would end it, but because it excludes death, because it is still there beneath death, a presence in the depths of absence, an inexorable day on which all the days rise and fall. (PF 324, 336–337)

The intelligibility of the world has its origin in our power of distancing ourselves from the immediacy of things, and that is to say, ultimately, in our awareness of death. Human existence, as an existence founded on language, is the 'life of the Spirit', that 'life that carries death, and that maintains itself in it', in the phrase from Hegel that

---

11 In 'The Paradox of Aytré', we find the same accusation: language and understanding carry with them a 'fundamental dispossession, this fatality such that I am always separated from myself, unable to adhere to anything, compelled to allow the original silence to slide between myself and what happens to me, this silence of consciousness by which there comes to each of my moments the meaning (*le sens*) that dispossesses me of it' (PF 75, 70).

recurs as a *leitmotif* in the essay. But the death or the nothingness on the basis of which things acquire their signification can, under certain conditions, come into doubt. This is here said to take place in the encounter with 'existence', that gives rise to 'anxiety'.[12] For the exposition of these terms, the passage refers to Emmanuel Levinas, but it is a recurrent theme in Blanchot, and one can come more directly to the sense that it has here by turning to 'The Reading of Kafka', the opening essay of *La Part du feu*, and also the one that is textually and thematically closest to 'Literature and the Right to Death':

> Such is the origin of our anxiety. It does not only come from this nothingness from which, we are told, human reality would emerge and then fall back into; it comes from the fear that this refuge could be taken from us, that there is not nothing, that nothing is still a kind of being (*qu'il n'y ait pas rien, que ce rien ne soit encore de l'être*) [. . .] If the night, suddenly, is put in doubt, then there is no longer either day or night, there is nothing more than a vague, crepuscular light, which is at one moment a reminder of the day, at the next a regret for the night, in one sense, the end of the sun, in another, the sun of the end. Existence is interminable, a mere indeterminate, and we do not know if we are excluded from it (and this is why we search in vain for some firm point of reference) or forever enclosed in it (and thus we turn desperately towards the outside). This existence is an exile in the strong sense of the word: we are not there, we are elsewhere there, and we never cease to be there. (PF 16–17, 8–9)

These remarks advance beyond the status of commentary, to summarize a more general predicament, in which we can recognize precisely the 'condemnation' that we have seen associated with language in

---

12 The reference is to Levinas, *De l'Existence à l'existant*. Second Edition. Paris: Vrin, 1963. (First edition, 1947). On the Blanchot–Levinas relation in this connection, see Leslie Hill, *Maurice Blanchot: Extreme Contemporary*. London: Routledge, 1997, Chapter 3; and Simon Critchley, *Very Little – Almost Nothing: Death, Philosophy, Literature*. London: Routledge, 1997.

'Literature and the Right to Death'.¹³ Kafka's stories are here taken to represent, not a particular (pessimistic) vision of the world, but rather the possibility of an experience deprived of the resources of negation. This privation, Blanchot suggests in 'Literature and the Right to Death', stems from an ambiguity inherent in negation itself:

> If we call this power negation, irreality or death, then at one moment, death, negation or irreality, working in the depth of language, announces the advent of truth in the world, the construction of intelligible being, meaning forming itself. But all at once, the sign changes: meaning no longer represents the marvel of understanding, but refers us to the nothingness of death, and intelligible being only signifies the refusal of existence, and the absolute concern for truth reveals itself to be the impossibility of truly acting. (PF 330–331, 344)

The uncovering of the 'ambiguity of the negative' is not presented as a critique, in the sense of a dismantling of a false construction. The weakness in the foundation is not something that is demonstrated, and in this way acquired as a negative knowledge. It represents only the possibility of a transformation. 'All at once, the sign changes', and the power of language to reveal an intelligible world assumes another aspect. The totality of the evidence given to the life that 'endures death and maintains itself in it' suddenly reverses its signification, becoming an enclosure or an exile. The dispossession of existence appears, then, not so much as the truth of things, but as a permanent latency contained in negation or death as the source of

---

13 I cite in the original here a dense sentence from the passage above, to indicate its resonance with the earlier passage. Blanchot writes: '*Si la nuit, soudain, est mise en doute, alors il n'y a plus ni jour ni nuit, il n'y a plus qu'une lumière vague, crépusculaire, qui est tantôt souvenir du jour, tantôt regret de la nuit, fin du soleil and soleil de la fin*'. In the passage cited earlier from 'Literature and the Right to Death', Blanchot writes that man finds himself enclosed within the light because the light is endless, and hence without issue, because 'the end is itself light, because it was from the end of beings that their signification (which is being) had come' (PF 313, 323). Signification is the 'end of the sun' because there is no longer a possible encounter with things in the natural light of perception. Rather, our vision is made possible by 'the sun of the end' (*le soleil de la fin*), that is to say, that light of meaning granted by the 'end' (*la fin*, i.e. their death or destruction).

our understanding, capable at any moment of voiding the constructions to which it has given rise.

Since our concern, in reading 'Literature and the Right to Death', has been to sketch out the most general schema of Blanchot's thought, we have had to confine ourselves to one path through this very complex text: in particular, the wealth of content on poetry and literature, primarily referring to questions of poetics in France in the nineteenth and twentieth centuries, has been elided. It is not incidental, however, that the thought is unfolded in the closest proximity to a reflection on literature. In order to suggest, at least in general terms, how these two dimensions are articulated, we can turn to the last words of the text:

> In this initial double meaning, which is situated in the depth of all language as a still unknown condemnation and a still invisible fortune, literature finds its origin, for it is the form chosen by this double meaning to manifest itself behind the meaning and the value of words, and the question that [this double meaning] poses is the question that is posed by literature. (PF 331, 344)

Let us unfold a little some of the elements contained in this very precise and complex statement. The initial ambiguity 'situated in the depth of all language' is at once a 'condemnation' and a 'fortune' (*un bonheur*, the sense of which in this context is closer to a 'chance' or even a 'gift' than to 'happiness'). Under both of these aspects, it remains unknown to us: it is 'a still unknown condemnation and a still invisible fortune' – the 'still', it would seem, implies that this is not necessarily the case. We have begun to see the form taken by the condemnation, in the 'exile' in which we can find ourselves at any moment, but which remains unknown to us as long as we lead 'the life of the spirit', holding and maintaining ourselves in death. The positivity (*le bonheur*) that is here balanced against this condemnation corresponds to a sequence of figures and verbal motifs such as lightness, the gift and grace, which never fail, even if only momentarily, to open the prospect of a sudden and unexpected reversal within the apparently unremittingly negative movement of Blanchot's texts. The positivity that Blanchot continues to accord to literature belongs in this sequence: if it is 'still invisible', it may remain so, one can suppose, as long as literature and art are understood and appreciated as what they are not – as an excellence of 'work', as a meaning determined in relation to a world that is in the process of accomplishing itself.

II

In its style, *L'Espace littéraire* is less brilliant and paradoxical than *La Part du feu*: its movement is less rapid, more meditative, at times incantatory. There is a high degree of consistency in the language and the themes of the work, and the overall impression is of greater unity than in the preceding collections. Nonetheless, the conceptual organization of the work is not easily accessible, and this no doubt has something to do with the fact that this extraordinary work has had relatively little influence in the wider field of literary criticism. The sequential movement is not particularly marked, and there is little indication as to how the various parts of the work stand in relation to each other. Some texts are closer to the critical format, while others make use of narrative and mythic elements, and this alternation is never justified or thematized. More than anything else, however, the reception of the work has been stalled by the fact some of its central concerns do not appear to belong to any recognizable area of inquiry. The opening text associates the act of writing with a particular experience, termed 'essential solitude', the various dimensions of which it assembles. The same description reappears in a number of subsequent texts, under other designations (the 'original experience', 'inspiration', 'the other night'). The hypnotic immediacy that such descriptions acquire is one of the most remarkable accomplishments of *L'Espace littéraire*. But their status is not easy to determine. The primary characteristic of the experience is that it is without a subject, that it takes place at an interval from any consciousness or memory, and so, one must assume, there can be no claim to knowledge. Nonetheless, the fact that the experience can be presented at all supposes that it is in some measure accessible to language, and thereby that it has a mediate relation to knowledge, at least to the extent of modifying our ordinary understanding of the self and demanding that we recognize its limits.

In order to critically engage with the claims of the text at the descriptive or cognitive level, it is necessary to approach the philosophical thought that informs it. This thought is essentially a continuation and an elaboration of the reflection on language and negation that we have been working out in reading 'Literature and the Right to Death.' We can see how the description of 'essential solitude' supposes and advances this thought by turning to the first of the four 'Annexes' attached to *L'Espace littéraire*, a text entitled 'Essential Solitude and Solitude in the World'. This text – one of the few not published prior to the book – is the extension of a footnote to 'The Essential Solitude'.[14] Although only a couple of pages long, and presented as a fragment, it is the most direct statement of the conceptual assumptions of *L'Espace littéraire*.

The guiding philosophical topic here is not language as it was in 'Literature and the Right to Death', but, rather, the self in its relation to the world. In a rare direct reference, Blanchot evokes the thought of Heidegger in introducing a determination of what it is to be 'at the level of the world' – an expression which here designates what *Being and Time* describes as 'everydayness', the mode of being in which we are engaged in practical and cognitive tasks, and in relations with others:

> When I am *at the level of the world*, there where there are also things and beings, being is profoundly dissimulated (as Heidegger has invited us to think). This dissimulation can become work, negation. 'I am' (in the world) tends to signify that I am only if I can separate myself from being. [. . .] We negate being – or, to clarify with reference to a particular case, we negate, we transform nature – and, in this negation, which is work and time, beings come to accomplishment and men elevate themselves to the freedom of the 'I am'. What makes me into the self that I am is this decision to be as separated from being, to be without being, to be that which owes nothing to being, that which has its power from the refusal of being, to be absolutely 'de-natured,' absolutely separate, absolutely absolute. (EL 337–338, 252, Blanchot's italics)

The passage is characteristic in its strange mixture of fidelity to certain details of Heidegger's texts, rendered with expert terminological

---

14 The situation of four texts in the margin of the work is not explained beyond the title 'Annexes', under which they are gathered. If nothing else, however, this arrangement signals a certain unity of intention to the other texts – 'L'Espace littéraire' proper – to which, for one reason or another, these texts did not belong.

precision, and moments of striking heterodoxy. The idea that being is 'protected' by its dissimulation in the world, for example, alludes to the interplay between sheltering and concealment, *bergen* and *verbergen* in Heidegger: as concealed (*verborgen*), being is also sheltered, *geborgen* (cf. *Holzwege*, 265). On the other hand, the next step, that 'this dissimulation can become work, negation' recalls much more the Hegelian terminology that we have seen at work in 'Literature and the Right to Death'. In a later text, Blanchot remarks that Heidegger does not recognize the philosophical resources of negation (A 107). This suggests that the merging of the two threads is worth pursuing, and reflects Blanchot's philosophical assumptions more generally.

The actual conception of what it is to be 'at the level of the world' in Blanchot – that is to say, of the human in its practical and cognitive activities – comes not so much from the analysis of *Dasein* in *Being and Time*, I would suggest, as from Hegel – and indeed not so much Hegel as the streamlined, functionalized version of Hegel worked out in Kojève's lectures. This folding of Hegel into Heidegger entails some terminological tension, above all around the vexed word 'being'. When Blanchot founds the self upon the possibility of a separation from 'being', then it is surely the Hegelian sense of the word that is meant, rather than the Heideggerean sense. The 'being' from which the self has to be able to separate itself, in order to 'be', is *given being*, that which is referred to as 'the real' by Kojève, when he writes that for Hegel:

> Freedom is the realization and the manifestation of negativity. It consists in the act of negating the real in its given structure and of maintaining this negation in the form of work.[15]

The activity of the self in the world is the negation of 'being', in the sense of what is merely there, independent of the self. A state of affairs, by which the self would otherwise be limited – a natural obstacle or an adverse circumstance, for example – is overcome by the negation of work. The negation of the given is not, however, confined to the mastery of the environment, to production and technological

---

15 *Introduction à la lecture de Hegel: leçons sur la* Phénoménologie de l'Esprit. Ed. Raymond Queneau. Paris: Gallimard, 1947, 555.

advance. If the subject simply imposed its will upon the world, then it would itself be like a natural, given process. The self is not 'natural', however, because it is defined by its refusal to assume substantial being, to rest in a definite character. It is important to recognize the extent to which this conception of the self is taken over by Blanchot. Certainly, it is not a matter of a historical fidelity (of a kind of 'Hegelianism'), but elements of the Hegelian conception are consistently appropriated and deployed by Blanchot in order to circumscribe the mode of being of the self in the world. In a condensed formulation that reappears at various points in this work, the self as negativity is grasped as 'being without being' (*être sans être*). In the work of freedom the self makes itself what it is through the contestation of *all* the realities that would give one a fixed, substantial reality (i.e. 'being'). As in Hegel/Kojève, this contestation is here identified with the process of history. The self confronts 'being' not only in the external physical world, but also in the form of social, political and legal arrangements, in the form of representations and beliefs. The work of freeing oneself from these limitations cannot be carried out solely on an individual basis, since their negation entails the transformation of society. Hence, Blanchot writes:

> This power by which I affirm myself in negating being is only real, however, in the community of all, in the common movement of work and of the work of time. 'I am', as the decision to be without being, only has truth because this decision that I make is founded in the community, because it accomplishes itself in the movement that it makes possible and that in turn makes it real: this reality is always historical, it is the world which is always the realization of the world. (338, 251–252)

It is essential to see that the conception of the self that is being elaborated here – the 'I am' that comes to be in negating itself – refers to the free rational self, not to the empirical self, with its particularity and its quest for personal satisfaction. In other words, it is not a matter of describing the experience of the self, in its moment to moment reality, but of grasping conceptually the demand to which this self submits when it takes part in work, in knowledge and in political action. The claim is not, then, that the particular self is conditioned by its historical environment, but that the self, in its potentiality for freedom, depends for its reality upon a historical process. Again, the claim is close to that in Hegel, where the self only has freedom and history in the true sense inasmuch as it shares in the movement of the universal self that Hegel calls Spirit (*Geist*) – the demands of which are in many respects contrary to the interests and desires of the actual self, as Hegel observes in the introduction to the *Philosophy of History*, when he speaks of the 'cunning of reason', making use of human passions for its own purposes.

The historical picture, too, is constructed with elements of the Hegelian conception. In Blanchot, the modern age tends to appear as something like the completion of the historical process announced in the *Phenomenology of Spirit*. This assumption is represented in the present text in the following sentence, which sums up its 'Hegelian' doctrine:

> When being is absent, when nothingness becomes a power, man is fully historical (*Quand l'être manque, quand le néant devient pouvoir, l'homme est pleinement historique*). (339, 252)

Human society is 'fully historical' from the moment that it corresponds to the essence of freedom in no longer affirming any kind of substantial principle, any kind of eternal truth. At this moment, announced and symbolized by the figure of Hegel, our manner of being in the world – as a power of negation – is fully recognized and assumed. Henceforth, 'being is absent': every reality, every principle, is now essentially provisional, illuminated for us by its future negation or transformation. This realization effectively transposes the theory of language in 'Literature and the Right to Death' to the historical plane. As language is able to name things on the basis of their possible negation, so the modern self encounters reality only in view of its future negation, in the course of the transformation of the world. This 'virtual' status of all reality is a *historical* accomplishment; it comes to assume this aspect in the process of philosophical reflection and critique, which moves to assure the dissolution of any inherited guarantee, of any sense-granting ground (a God, for example). In assuming this evidence – that is, in deciding 'to be without being' – the human sets itself up as the absolute, recognizes itself as free of any given absolute principle, and initiates the final stage in its progressive realization.

I have underlined that the structure of the self as negativity does not correspond to the immediate experience of the self as such. It is, however, precisely the *experience* of negativity that is at issue in the contrast of 'essential solitude' and 'solitude in the world'. 'Solitude in the world' represents the experience that the self can have of the negativity that founds it. Such an experience, Blanchot suggests, corresponds to 'what one generally calls anxiety (*angoisse*)' (338, 252). This is no doubt a reference to the vogue of existentialism, in particular, the reception of Kierkegaard and the appropriation of his treatment of anxiety in Sartre's *Being and Nothingness*. The avoidance of this term, which as we have seen, appears in Blanchot's earlier works, may reflect a sense of its exhaustion in the wake of the existentialist moment in the 1940s and 1950s. It returns in *Le Pas au-delà* and *L'Écriture du désastre*. But there is also a conceptual differentiation at work here. For Sartre, anxiety is the experience the self has of its lack of 'essence', of the radical freedom that compels it always to be different from anything that would give it the identity of a determination. As unsettling as it may be for the self to experience itself as neither having nor being able to give itself definitive identity, this vertiginous experience is the condition of a truly free existence, and it is what ultimately allows us to become 'fully historical', to occupy a world in which all things are understood to be in a movement of becoming. To interpret anxiety in this way, Blanchot writes, is to 'cover over the essential' (338, 252). Let us turn, then, to the difficult and abstract passage that proposes to lead us to 'the essential'. By a characteristic rhetorical turn, it begins with a question, which then modulates into an affirmation:

> But when being is absent – is it absent? When being is absent, does that mean that this absence owes nothing at all to being, or is it not perhaps that being is still the ground of the absence of being, that there is still being, when there is nothing? When being is absent, being is merely profoundly dissimulated. If one approaches this absence, such as it is present in 'the essential solitude', what one encounters is being, rendered present by the absence of being, no longer being dissimulated, but being *as* dissimulated: dissimulation itself. ('*Mais quand l'être manque, l'être manque-t-il? Quand l'être manque, cela signifie-t-il que ce manque ne doive rien à l'être ou bien ne serait-il pas l'être qui est au fond de*

l'absence de l'être, ce qu'il y a encore d'être quand il n'y a rien? Quand l'être manque, l'être n'est encore que profondément dissimulée. Pour celui qui s'approche de ce manque, tel qu'il est présent dans "la solitude essentielle", ce qui vient à sa rencontre, c'est l'être que l'absence d'être rend présent, non plus l'être dissimulé, mais l'être en tant que dissimulé: la dissimulation elle-même.'). (339–340, 252–253)

One sees here the tendency of Blanchot's writing to move towards hermetic condensation: it is essential to realize, however, that, in this condensation, the content of previous analyses is implied and retained. Under what is here simply designated as the 'absence of being', as we have seen, there has been gathered together the enabling assumptions of the modern historical consciousness. 'Essential solitude', then, is an experience in which the power of 'absence' comes into doubt: as such it occupies precisely the position given to anxiety (via Levinas and Kafka) in *La Part du feu*. The language remains similar to the earlier texts: there as here what is encountered is a limit to absence, considered as the condition of freedom and power, a presence that is still there in the depths of absence (cf. PF 324, 337). What is different in the present version is its location within a conceptual construction that draws on Heidegger. The term 'dissimulation' invokes the Heideggerean interpretation of being as concealment, and a subsequent passage confirms the reference to 'On the Essence of Truth' in spelling out a sequence of alternative possible situations that follows closely the exposition of this work:[16]

In the tranquility of everyday life, dissimulation dissimulates itself. In action, in the true action that is that of the work of history, dissimulation tends to become negation (the negative is our task, and this task is the task of truth). But in what we are calling essential solitude, dissimulation tends to appear. (340, 253)

For Heidegger, being (*das Sein*) conceals itself, as part of the opening up of world that allows beings (*das Seiende*) to appear, but in the course of ordinary life, this concealment is itself forgotten,

---

16 Compare *Pathmarks*, 148–149.

is not allowed its own reserve in the world – hence 'dissimulation dissimulates itself'.[17] The concealment of being in this sense is associated with the pressure of need and habit, the flattening out introduced by the world of the everyday and the familiar. But this attrition of the original opening, to which, at some level, we necessarily remain attuned, is not overcome in the self-conscious and controlled discourse of philosophy. On the contrary, it is reinforced by the more profound forgetting of being that Heidegger sees prevailing throughout the metaphysical tradition and reaching its apex in the modern epoch, with the rise of what he calls the metaphysics of subjectivity. At this historical moment, man takes himself as 'the measure for all that is', and can only allow to be that which is represented to the subject.[18] Heidegger's critical attitude towards the modern epoch corresponds to the movement with which Blanchot is primarily concerned, to the 'true action that is the work of history', the moment at which 'dissimulation becomes negation', at which 'being is absent' (the last expression, as I have remarked, is not in conformity with Heidegger's usage, but the historical picture is certainly similar).

In contrast: in 'the essential solitude, what one encounters is being, rendered present by the absence of being, no longer being dissimulated, but being *as* dissimulated: dissimulation itself' (cited above). The distinction between the dissimulation of being and being *as* dissimulation is deployed by Heidegger to make the transition from the human tendency to turn away from the ontological dimension to a movement of concealment proper to being itself, an untruth belonging to the essence of truth (cf. *Pathmarks*, 148–149). In *L'Espace littéraire*, the ambiguity of the negative is articulated within this structure. In reading the 'Literature and the Right to Death' and the 'Annex' text, we have seen that, for Blanchot, the absence of being opens up and prevails over the human relation to the self and to things, and that it does so in a more explicit and conscious way in the modern age, as the self understands itself as free reason and its relation to the world takes the form of mastery and power. In taking advantage

---

17 'Die Ansässigkeit im Gängigen ist aber in sich das Nichtwaltenlassen der Verbergung des Verborgenen' (Wegmarken 195).
18 *Pathmarks*, 149–150.

The Ambiguity of the Negative 89

of our distance from things in order to see everything as provisional and subject to modification, we have made absence into a power at our disposal. In this way, however, we have contracted a relation to absence 'itself', to 'that which is when there is nothing, which is no longer when there is something' (EL 26, 30). This is the point at which the Heideggerean structure intervenes. In deriving freedom, mastery and future from the power *not* to be (not to be anything definite, anything fixed), we make nothingness into a power: but this is only possible in concealing absence as inertia (*le désoeuvrement*). This inertia, by its dissimulation, allows us to turn away from it, but we continue to be bound to it, at all points, from the fact that we relate to the world in the human way, as language and possibility. This is why, behind the self, the 'I' that is active in the world, there is the 'essential solitude', in which 'dissimulation tends to appear' (340, 253).[19]

The opening text of *L'Espace littéraire*, entitled 'The Essential Solitude' (from which the 'Annex' that we have been reading is a kind of extended explanatory note), describes the transformation of all the essential categories of experience as the self encounters the presence of 'the nothing'; these categories are then not voided simply, but given *without negation*. Then 'here' becomes 'nowhere' and yet nowhere is also here; the 'I' recognizes itself as 'someone' or 'the he' (*le il*); the power of the gaze becomes fascination; and the synthetic and narrative movement of temporal experience stalls in a 'dead time', in the time of repetition (*le recommencement, le ressassement eternel*). In *L'Entretien infini*, the analysis will be restated as a division of the self between the dimension of possibility opened up by the power of the negative and the dimension of impossibility, in which the self is engaged by the excess of this negativity over the power of the self to make use of it. Our trajectory to this point has enabled us to recognize that the privation of world, self and time whose description occupies so much of Blanchot's work, does not represent a pathological condition, at the border of the self and consciousness, but has its origin in the specifically human mode of relation to the world. The 'essential

---

19 The same structure can be traced in the chapter entitled 'The Outside, the Night' (EL V i): the space of the day (*le jour*) is bounded and made possible by the night. The 'night' here signifies the end (*la fin*) towards which work and language move, and whose sighting in advance makes them possible, by relating them to the future of their accomplishment: but this night opens on to what Blanchot calls 'the other night', the night as the absence of the end, the 'outside' from which there is no exit.

solitude' does not *describe* an experience that is simply 'there' to be described, for the one who has seen it, known it or hypothesized it. For this 'knowledge' only becomes possible on the basis of the presuppositions of the ontological thought, which are not those of a specific branch of science (such as psychology, for example) which, in the ordinary course of things, one would expect to record and systematize such experience. It is only because the ambiguity of the negative has been understood *in advance* that the description is able to gather together the phenomena, to see them in their inter-relation and their significance, which is to say, effectively, to see them at all. From the point of view of knowledge and understanding, which takes it as axiomatic that our mode of being in the world is essentially that of possibility – such evidence has to appear as a *deficient* phenomenon, and this initial interpretation will necessarily condition all discourse on the subject. Blanchot's description, by contrast, supposes that impossibility is an original dimension of the self, even, as he writes in a later text, our 'ultimate dimension' (EI 68, 48).

III

As we have begun to see, Blanchot's thought develops by the repetition of the same questions, the same insights, under different forms. In each repetition, however, certain aspects come into view from a new angle. The philosophical position that we have been exploring in these texts cannot be fully grasped without considering Blanchot's writings on death, a topic which constitutes one of the essential paths of his thought. We can gain a first overview of the problematic by turning to a passage from 'The Original Experience' (EL VII.iii). From Hegel, Blanchot writes, we have learned that it is only 'the resolute confrontation with death that allows man to become the active nothingness, capable of negating and transforming natural reality, of struggle, work, knowing and of being historical' (EL 322, 240). Death is 'the magical force, the absolute power that becomes the work of truth in the world, that brings negation to reality, form to the unformed, the end to the indefinite' (ibid):

> That, in man, everything should be possibility, such an affirmation requires first that death, without which man could not form a whole, nor exist in view of a whole, should itself be a power,

should be possible, should be that which makes everything possible, that which makes the whole possible. (322, 240)

The human is 'possibility' in the sense that this term expresses the absence of necessity, the absence of determination: 'that in man everything should be possibility' signifies that nothing in man is absolutely given, that in no respect is the being of man determined in advance, exclusive of possible modification, and therefore, that the human is the 'being without being'.[20] In consequence, in the world of the day (*le jour*) that we inhabit, things are not merely an indifferent presence (*Vorhandenheit* in Heidegger); what is given takes on its sense *for* us, for our capacity of work and transformation. That we can be such a power, however, requires that we first of all have taken possession of death, through our anticipatory understanding of death as possibility. The continuity with the texts that we have read to this point is readily apparent: the anticipatory awareness of death supplies the initial 'absence' or 'nothingness' (the ontological truth) on the basis of which things can be given at a distance, mediated by their absence.

The ambiguity of the negative now reappears in the relation to death. Death is the ground on which we stand but it is also the absence of ground; it is 'the point from which the foundation can be given', and at the same time, it is 'the pure void without importance' – 'but always the one and the other at the same time, the interlacing of the yes and the no, the flux and reflux of the essential ambiguity' (321, 239). The specific human relation to death makes us into a creature of possibility, into a force that transforms all that is given, but it also exposes us to the danger of a 'radical reversal' – not in the sense that one dies simply, and thereby loses all one's possibilities, but in the sense that this event does not belong to the self: 'one dies always other than oneself, with the neutrality and the impersonality of an eternal *he*' (323, 241).

This exposition appears close to the end of *L'Espace littéraire*, at a moment at which the reflection pauses and restates its leading question – 'what it means that we have art' (cf. 321, 239). It prepares the

---

20 The suggestion that the being of the human can be gathered together under the term 'possibility' will be more fully worked out in a later text, 'The Great Refusal' in *L'Entretien infini* (EI I.iv).

conclusion that the very existence of art and literature signifies that we have 'a relation with death which is not that of possibility' (323, 241). The 'radical reversal' contained within the possibility of death, is 'the original experience on which the work has to touch, on which it closes itself, and which risks constantly to close over it and to destroy it' (ibid). We can see these statements as a new form – a repetition – of the claim, in 'Literature and the Right to Death', that literature has its origin in the ambiguity of the negative ('the double meaning of meaning'). In order to see how this new version can help us to grasp the position, it is necessary to examine more closely what it means that we have another relation with death than possibility.

To this end, I turn now to Section IV of *L'Espace littéraire*, entitled 'The Work and the Space of Death', in which a meditation on death is pursued through and alongside studies of Kafka, Mallarmé and Rilke. In particular, I will examine more closely the first text in this section, entitled 'The Possible Death' ('La Mort possible', EL IV.i).

I begin at the point at which the text turns more directly to the philosophical questioning of death as a phenomenon (with the subsection entitled 'Can I Die?').[21] The question here is that of the *certainty* of death. At one level – at the level of the world – death can be unproblematically considered as a certainty. As such, it can be calculated upon in a multitude of circumstances, and from a number of points of view, moral, strategic, economic, psychological and theological. This mundane certainty had already been put in question, however, in the famous chapters on death in Heidegger's *Being and Time*. One of the key propositions of this text is that death is not seen in its genuine character as a phenomenon when it is seen as a fact, along with all kinds of other facts, known in the space of objectivity. Death only has its being in its relation to the self: 'Death, inasmuch

---

21 The textual history of 'The Possible Death' reveals that it is a composite piece. It was first published in November of 1952, in *Critique* ('The Essential Solitude' was first published in January of 1953, in the *NRF*, and there is considerable resonance between their inquiries). For its publication in *L'Espace littéraire*, Blanchot added a section entitled 'The Word Experience', which had first appeared as part of the essay entitled 'A Toute extremité', published in the NRF in February of 1955, the remainder of which was collected as a separate essay in *Le Livre à venir*. One section of 'Death as Possibility' – the rather idiosyncratic discussion of Kafka, entitled 'To Die Content' ('La Mort contente') – was reprinted separately in the much later collection, *De Kafka à Kafka* (1981).

as it "is', is always mine'.²² The certainty of death is not necessarily diminished when it is seen from this point of view, but it is no longer the certainty of a fact – rather that of a demand, in assuming which we accede to a more genuine accord with our actual situation. The recognition that death is at every moment possible is the precondition of an authentic existence, since it compels one to take distance from the self-understanding that circulates within the everyday world, and to choose and make one's own one of the definite possibilities that are offered to us (cf. *Being and Time*, Sections 74–75).

There can be no doubt that Blanchot's thought is decisively marked by Heidegger, here, as on so many other points, and one could well proceed by comparing and opposing the two works. But Blanchot's approach to this question is ultimately independent, and it is possible to grasp its main outlines in its own terms. One notes, for example, that the questioning of death as a certainty takes a somewhat different path. The phenomenological clarification of Heidegger is diverted in an epistemological direction, by an emphasis on the question of verification. Death, Blanchot claims, does not quite fulfil the criteria of factuality, since it cannot be experienced in the first person (the point, it should be noted, supposes the Heideggerean determination of death as a phenomenon that belongs properly to the self, since otherwise its factual status could, of course, be established by empirical evidence). Since death can never be given in evidence to self-consciousness, it is 'without truth, or at least, it does not have the truth that we test and confirm in the world (*la verité que nous éprouvons dans le monde*)'. ²³ As something that I can only imagine, and not experience, not test and confirm (*éprouver*), death always retains an element of unreality:

> What makes me disappear from the world cannot find its guarantee in the world, and is therefore, in a certain manner, without guarantee, is not sure. This is why one cannot have a relation to death that is characterized by a true certainty. No one is sure of dying, no one doubts death, and yet one can only think certain

---

22 *Being and Time*. Trans. John Macquarie and Edward Robinson. NY: Harper and Row, 1962, Section 47.
23 For similar versions of this argument, see also 'The Reading of Kafka', the opening essay of *La Part du feu* (especially PF 15–19, 7–11), 'Literature and the Right to Death' (PF 324–325, 337–338) and also the essay on Leiris (PF 245–246, 252–253).

death in a doubtful way, for to think death is to introduce the supremely doubtful into thought, the erosion of the non-certain [...] This shows already that, if in general people do not think of death, if they tend to evade it, then without doubt this is to flee it and to hide themselves from it (*se dissimuler à elle*), but this evasion is only possible because death is itself a perpetual flight before death, because it is the depth of dissimulation. Thus, to dissimulate oneself from it is, in a certain manner, to dissimulate oneself in it. (EL 117, 95)

Once the certainty of death is put in question, the psychology of the human relation to death appears in a new light. Timidity and avoidance in face of the fact of death are no longer a weakness stemming from the passion for life, but reflect the evasive character of death itself. Death does not grant us the distance from which we could come to terms with it. In fleeing it, one stands already within its sphere of influence. '[D]eath is itself a perpetual flight before death, because it is the depth of dissimulation' (*la profondeur de la dissimulation*).

The sentence exemplifies the hermetic 'method' of *L'Espace littéraire*, in which verbal repetitions constantly signal links to other parts of the text – especially, as here, in the most condensed and difficult formulations.[24] The term 'dissimulation', as we have seen in the 'Annex' text, has been used to translate the Heideggerean term for the concealment of being (*die Verbergung*) (cf. *Pathmarks*, 148–150). Now we begin to see that the same structure can also be located within the relation to death. The distinctive human relation to the world is opened up by the anticipatory possession of death, but Blanchot will also suggest that this possession can be maintained only by evading death as 'the supremely doubtful'. This evasion, moreover, should not be considered as the mark of a fearful or 'inauthentic' mode of being. Rather, it is allowed and encouraged by death itself, as 'the depth of dissimulation'.

We have seen how, in its restatement of the relation to the negative, *L'Espace littéraire* introduces a significant modification of the scheme of 'Literature and the Right to Death'. The questioning of

---

24 Another example: the figure of 'flight' (*la fuite*) reappears in more extended developments in a number of later texts, notably in 'La Question la plus profonde' (cf. EI 24–31, 19–23) and in 'La Chute: la fuite' (A 228–235, 201–207).

all metaphysical principles in the modern period amounts to an adherence, a commitment to the absence of givens as the guarantee of human freedom and openness to the future. The 'nothing' at the ground of the free and transformative relation to the world has to be won, wrested from the imposition of religious and metaphysical positivity. The historical dimension of the question of death in 'La Mort possible' follows out the implications of this point. The question of our relation to death, Blanchot suggests, only appears in its full significance in the modern period. No doubt death has always been a locus of mystery and fear, but in 'the great religious systems', death is primarily the pathway to the larger world and therefore its elusive character, as a 'fact without truth', is not posed as a problem for thought (cf. EL 118, 96). Modern subjectivity, however, in deriving the prospect of a properly human world from its mortal condition, assigns itself the task of making death its own:

> As soon as he gathers himself entirely to himself, in the certainty of his mortal condition, the concern of man becomes to make death possible. It is no longer enough for him to be mortal, he understands that he must become mortal, he must be doubly mortal – sovereignly, extremely mortal. This is his human vocation. Death, in the horizon of the human, is not what is given, it is what is to be accomplished: a task, something which we seize actively, and which becomes the source of our activity and of our mastery. That man dies is nothing in itself: but man *is* on the basis of his death, he binds himself powerfully to his death, by a link of which he is himself judge, he makes his death, makes himself mortal – and thereby, he gives himself the power to act, and gives to his acts their sense and their truth. The decision to be without being (*la décision d'être sans être*) is precisely this possibility of death. Hegel, Nietzsche and Heidegger, the three thinkers who seek to grasp the sense of this decision and who, for this reason, seem most clearly to illuminate the destiny of modern man, all tend to make death possible, whatever else may oppose them. (118, 96)

'The decision to be without being is precisely this possibility of death', Blanchot writes. The decision 'to be without being' – to assume our own absence of foundation, to become 'entirely possibility' – requires that we are capable of death. The sense of this ultimate possibility seems at first to be ethical or existential, referring to a confrontation and a decision that concerns the individual. Such is the case in Heidegger's discussion of 'being-towards-death' in *Being and Time*; and although the context is somewhat different, more concerned with power and conflict than with authentic self-understanding, the same is true of Hegel (i.e. of Hegel/Kojève). By the power of dying, Hegel proposes, we show that we are superior to all external constraints. Nothing can be an absolute given for me, if I am prepared to give up my life in order that it not be the case.[25] In the passage we have just read, however, Blanchot seems to suggest that this struggle is also contested at the conceptual level, in the interpretation of death. Hegel, Nietzsche and Heidegger are invoked as the three thinkers who mark the major stages in the ongoing philosophical engagement with atheism and radical freedom, and all 'tend to make death possible'.[26]

At this point, the precise stance taken up by Blanchot's text towards this 'tendency' is difficult to decide. To say that these philosophers '*tend* to make death possible' implies that they can be considered as examples of a historical movement, that their attempts were partly dictated by their historical–metaphysical situation. To say that they 'tend *to make* death possible' is undoubtedly to imply that they impose a construction on the thing itself, that they cover over death as the 'erosion of the non-certain'. And yet if death is not possible, does this mean that the demand to 'be without being' that we have seen advanced as a consequential modern ethos, a rigorous response to non-foundation, is fallacious at ground? Is what is above called 'the human vocation' inherently contradictory, and condemned to failure?

The questions are worked out dramatically in the ensuing discussion of the figure of Kirilov, from Dostoyevsky's *The Devils*. Kirilov, an atheist and a sympathizer with nineteenth-century revolutionary

---

25 See Kojève, *Introduction à la lecture de Hegel*, 555–557.
26 In the essay 'The Thing' (first published in 1951, that is, during the period in which Blanchot would have been engaged in the reflections that led to *L'Espace littéraire*), Heidegger writes: 'To die means: to be capable of death as death. Only man dies in this sense. The animal perishes. It does not have death as death before itself or behind itself. Death is the shrine of the nothingness, of that which is in no respect a mere being, but which nonetheless has its own presence, and indeed has this as the mystery of being in itself.' *Vorträge und Aufsätze*. Pfullingen: Günther Neske, 1954, 171.

ideals, decides to commit suicide in order to demonstrate the ultimate freedom of humans from all religion and morality, which he sees as originating in the fear of death. Kirilov here seems to function as a synechdoche for Hegel, Nietzsche and Heidegger, a means of presenting the ground that these philosophers are here said to have in common, without embarking on the detailed analysis that this claim would require on the level of philosophical interpretation. In the novel, Kirilov is an ambiguous figure: he is idealistic, and there are suggestions that he conceives of his act as a Christ-like sacrifice, undertaken for the good of future humanity. On the other hand, the realism of the portrayal of his society and its institutions, and the complex but more conventional dramas of love and friendship in which his story is embedded, tend to relativize his thought, and reveal him as a young man led astray by the power of ideas, specifically, by the tendencies of the contemporary nihilism and atheism, to which Dostoyevsky himself was very much opposed. Blanchot disregards entirely these psychological and political dimensions of the novel, and appears, indeed, to give his entire assent to the logic of Kirilov, transposing the reasoning of the latter into his own philosophical language:

> If [Kirilov] dies freely, if he tests and proves to himself his freedom with his death, he will have attained the absolute, he will be this absolute, absolutely man, and there will be no absolute beyond him. (120, 97)
>
> Assuredly, if [Kirilov] succeeds in making death into a possibility that is his own, something purely human, he will have attained absolute freedom, he will have attained it as a man and he will have given it to humanity. (122, 99)

The commentary moves from this exposition of the thought towards what Kirilov 'wants', beyond the formulated intentions of the character himself. This thought behind the thought is explicated by Blanchot, as if assuming the voice of Kirilov, the suicide, in a series of questions:

> Can I commit suicide? (*Puis-je me donner la mort?*) Do I have the power to die? Up to what point can I advance freely into death, with full mastery of my freedom? Even where I decide to go to it, by an active and ideal resolution, is it not still that which comes

to me, and when I take hold of it, is it not still that which takes hold of me, dispossesses me, gives me over to the ungraspable? (121–122, 98).

Se donner la mort, the idiomatic expression for 'to commit suicide' in French, in its literal meaning ('to give oneself death') seems to compress what has been presented as the assignment of modern thought – to transform death by making it into the starting point from which all one's valuations, all one's actions, are decided. The questions that are posed here, it must be noted, do not concern the limits of human will and decision in face of the contingency of death. The doubt is not that, after all, it can still always come, that even the most rigorously willed suicide cannot succeed entirely in eliminating the element of chance. The question is whether it is possible to sustain a relation to this irreducible contingency that has the form of possibility. It is in this sense that the suicide seems to symbolize and put to the test the assumptions of modern thought in its appropriation of death as the ultimate possibility (and thus furnishes another sense in which one can consider modern thought as a 'nihilism').

For Blanchot, the insight of Dostoyevsky's text consists in its representation of the flaw in the notion of the freely chosen death. When Kirilov's last days are filled with vacillation, when he is discovered praying before the icon, it is not a sign of psychological weakness, but rather points to something like a logical error in the project of suicide. Suicide, Blanchot suggest, is not actually possible. Certainly, it takes place, but in order to properly see what it is that then takes place, we must realize that, in approaching death as the object of a task, to be carried out like other tasks, the suicide falsifies the sense of what death is:

> One cannot 'project' to kill oneself. This apparent project orients itself towards something which is never attained, towards a goal that cannot be aimed at: the end is what I cannot possibly take as an end. But this means that death withdraws from the time of work, from this time which is nonetheless death rendered active and capable. And this leads one to think that there are, so to speak, two deaths, one which circulates in words such as possibility and freedom, and which has the freedom to die and the power to risk one's life as its extreme horizon, and another

death which is out of our reach, which I cannot take hold of, which is not linked to *me* by any relation of any kind, which never comes, towards which I cannot go. (130, 103–104)

If, as Heidegger suggests, the phenomenon of death cannot be understood as a kind of fact in the world, neither can it adequately be conceived as the prospect that shows itself to me, as my death. In accordance with the pattern that has emerged in the course of these texts, it is not a matter of posing an alternative ('either-or'), but an ambiguity ('both-and'). It is certainly true that 'the freedom to die and the power to risk one's life' is 'the extreme horizon' of possibility: it is the most that I can possibly do, more cannot be asked of me. But in the character of Kirilov, we see that the one who would seek to take possession of this ultimate possibility does not remain himself: 'the one who wants to die does not die, loses the will to die, enters into the nocturnal fascination, dying in a passion without will' (131, 105).

These lines sketch out the traits of an experience that is portrayed through a number of figures, drawn from both fiction and literary history, in *L'Espace littéraire*. In 'the fascinated dispossession' of Kirilov, in the 'aimless passion' of Kleist, or in Nerval, wandering in the streets before his suicide, we are invited to see the reflection of the 'immense passivity of death' (127, 102). In 'The Outside, the Night', the same traits are encountered in the figure of Brekhounov, a wealthy merchant in Tolstoy who is lost in a storm, and who sets off to find help but whose movement becomes '*l'erreur de l'infini*', as in a labyrinth, where each step forward is a also a step back (EL 215–218, 164–167). In such figures, we see the encounter with the moment in the phenomenon of death that cannot be taken in charge in heroic action, in free sacrifice, nor even in acceptance and resignation. At this moment, death remains out of reach, is not linked to the self in any way whatsoever, is encountered only by the 'someone' who moves within the 'nocturnal space' of a movement without end (127, 102).

This experience is not merely what lies just over the 'extreme horizon'. It is not the limit of the human as possibility, the point at which the anticipatory possession of death is lost with the disintegration of the living organism. The relationship to death is engaged, not inasmuch as we are a living being (it is not an organic presentiment), but inasmuch as we relate to the world in the distinctive mode of the self, as freedom, mastery and futurity. This mode of being, we have seen, has its origin in the relationship to death. In entering into this relationship – that is, in speaking, in relating to things in the mode of possibility – we have also entered into a relation to the 'other death'; the 'he' that errs in the power of this death, therefore, discovers an essential part of what it is to be a self, and although Blanchot does not draw this conclusion, it follows from the analysis that it is only the human that enters into the space of the 'he'.[27]

It is at this point that we can begin to see the sense of the identification of literature with 'a relation with death which is not that of possibility' (323, 241). The connection returns in the final section of 'La Mort possible', entitled 'Art, Suicide'. As is characteristic of Blanchot, the reflection on art and literature is approached in terms of the relation of the writer to the work. This relation, it is suggested, can be understood by analogy with the paradox of suicide:

> [the artist] is linked to the work in the same strange manner as the suicide is to his death ([*l'artiste*] *est lié à l'oeuvre de la même étrange manière qu'est à la mort l'homme qui la prend pour fin*). (132, 105)

The action of the suicide, we have seen, contains an element of illusion: it carries out a task, aims at a result, but the whole process is disengaged from the reality of action because the 'object' does not ultimately lie within our sphere of effect. The suicide can only be accomplished by a 'leap' from the self-possession that disposes over life and death to the experience of death as the irreality of the indefinite, as the space where the end becomes the infinite, ever out of reach.

This 'leap' is the common term that links the two experiences. A number of texts in *L'Espace littéraire* describe the trajectory of the writer as a movement that leads outside the world, outside the self, to the situation where language is no longer in my power, where it is not I who speaks, where I am exiled from all possibility.[28] It is not quite the case, however, that the experience of the writer is simply equated with the mortal absence of the self that is glimpsed in the figure of the suicide. In the concluding passage of the text we have been

---

27 In order to approach this question, an important text would be 'The Birth of Art', A 9–20, 1–11.
28 See especially 'The Essential Solitude' and 'The Work and the Erring Speech' (EL I, III.i).

reading, Blanchot differentiates between the structure of the 'leap' in each case:

> The suicide is oriented towards this reversal, as towards its end. The work seeks it as its origin. This is a first difference. The suicide negates it, in a certain measure, does not take it into account, is only 'possible' in this refusal. Voluntary death is a refusal to see the other death, a kind of sovereign negligence, an alliance with the death that is visible intended to exclude the invisible death [. . .]. The expression 'I kill myself' suggests the split which is left out of account. The 'I' is a self in the plenitude of its action and its action, capable of acting sovereignly in relation to itself, always able to take itself in hand, and yet the one that is affected is not a self, is an other, so that when I commit suicide, it is perhaps 'I' who acts, but it is not me who is acted upon, and it is not my death either, not the death that I have chosen, that I have to die, but rather the one that I have refused and neglected, and which is itself this very negligence, perpetual flight and inertia.
>
> The work would like in a certain way to install itself in this *negligence*, to dwell there. An appeal comes to it from there. In spite of itself, it is attracted by what puts it absolutely to the test, by a risk in which everything is at stake, the essential risk, where being is at stake, where nothing withdraws, where the right and the power to die are in question. (133–134, 106–107)

In order to be carried through, the suicide has to ignore the other side of death, the death that belongs, not to me, but to 'someone', to the 'he'. If the suicide is 'oriented' towards this reversal, then it is not consciously so, but blindly, 'with a kind of sovereign negligence'. The work, by contrast, 'seeks' (*recherche*) this reversal, and 'would like' to establish a relation to the otherness of death; in so doing, it moves not towards its end, but towards its origin, towards the moment at which it first becomes possible: hence, elsewhere in the work, the claim that writing cannot begin until the writer belongs to the inertia in which language is not a power, in which it is 'only image, an imaginary language and the language of the imaginary' (EL 51, 48).

Blanchot's thought accompanies his readings of literary works, and develops alongside them: it is not 'theoretical' in the sense of being oriented towards a methodological definition of the object that is to be studied. It concerns rather the situation, the conceptual horizon, within which literary works take on their significance. This horizon becomes visible in the course of the philosophical interrogation of the foundations of our self-understanding as possibility, and of our possession of language as a means of knowing and representing the world. As we have seen throughout this study, the entry into the space of language, of possibility, is effected by the initial 'transcendence' towards death, and from this moment, the one who speaks and understands is bound to the ambiguity of the negative, to death as 'negligence, perpetual flight and inertia'. In relation to self, this death is an inert presence: it 'is not linked to *me* by any relation of any kind' (130, 106), but it is an essential thesis for Blanchot that 'dissimulation', that from which we can only turn away, is nonetheless present as a demand that weighs upon language and existence.[29] The literary activity has its origin in this demand: 'an appeal comes to work from there; it would like to install itself there'. Blanchot's critical texts illustrate the diversity of the paths and the figures by which this demand is encountered and negotiated. But a paradox separates this procedure from any kind of method of reading: the readings of the literary works are made possible by the elaboration of the ambiguity of the negative, but it is also the case that the literary phenomenon is the form in which this ambiguity becomes manifest. The pattern is circular – and at a number of points Blanchot acknowledges that this circularity is the condition of his thought (cf. EL 114, 93). The observation allows us to see the importance of the historical dimension of this thought, as the point of access into the circle. The self-understanding of the human as possibility is historical; the modern period is the one in which we take possession of the negative, at which 'nothingness becomes a power'; the demand upon thought is now to 'make death possible', but it is also the moment at which literature is experienced as a question, and the work becomes the infinite search for its origin. The convergence is one of the central points around which Blanchot's writings on literature turn, and it is one of the points at which literary studies would have to engage with Blanchot's work, if it is to encounter it at all.

---

29 Compare EI 111–112, 78–79.

5 Myth and Representation in Blanchot's Literary Criticism

I

One of the greatest difficulties presented by Blanchot's writings on literature is the intertwining of mythic, narrative and figural elements with critical, interpretive work. This means that one cannot definitely locate the texts in either the literary or the representational sphere of discourse. But nor can one solve the problem by considering these essays as 'literary' criticism, granting them a literary value to which academic studies generally make no claim, but also subtracting something thereby from the relevance of their statement to a discourse that is intended to establish a certain kind of knowledge. The 'mythic' elements in Blanchot's work – which make up so much of what is strange and difficult to place in *L'Espace littéraire* and *Le Livre à venir* – play an essential role in the articulation of the thought. The real problem in reading Blanchot in the context of literary studies is less the balance of poetic and representational elements than the articulation of a philosophical discourse concerned with the possibility of the literary work and a critical discourse, engaged with the phenomenon of literature, as this is encountered and experienced within the world.

Here we will begin with the poetics, the discourse on the work of art, on reading and writing. The main focus will be *L'Espace littéraire*, since this is the most concentrated presentation of the poetics, and much of what is developed there is then re-cast in later critical texts, especially in *Le Livre à venir*. I will begin, however, by looking at the idea of the work as it appears in *La Part du feu*, where in fact many of the elements of what is later worked out are already present – though noticeably without the mythic elements deployed in the later texts. At the end of 'The Myth of Mallarmé', Blanchot writes that what is 'most remarkable' in Mallarmé's writings on literature is 'the impersonal character, the kind of independent and absolute existence' that Mallarmé accords to the language of the literary work:

> This language does not suppose someone who expresses it, nor someone who hears it: it speaks itself and writes itself (*il se parle et s'écrit*). This is the condition of its authority. The book is the symbol of this autonomous subsistence: it goes beyond us, we cannot do anything to it, and we play almost no role in making it what it is. (PF 48, 41–42)

At this point, it is a matter of the exposition of the thought of 'the work' (*l'oeuvre*) as a key theme of *Mallarmé*. In a series of subsequent essays, however – in the texts entitled 'The Mystery in Letters' and 'The Paradox of Aytré' (both commenting on texts by Jean Paulhan), and again, in the essays on René Char and Hölderlin – a similar conception reappears: each time, the presentation resonates with the language of the writer to which the text is devoted, but in the course of the repetitions, it also comes to acquire the consistency of an autonomous reflection. Let us cite here the recapitulative statement that appears in the text entitled 'Pascal's Hand':

> We have seen, by the example of poets such as Mallarmé and Hölderlin, how, for them, language is not the simple power of speaking belonging to one gifted with this power, but claims to be anterior, both to the one who names and to what it names, even claiming that the one who speaks, the one who hears, and that which is said, only take on sense and existence from the original fact of language. (PF 254, 261–262)

This aspect of Blanchot's writing has attracted very little critical treatment, even within the scholarly studies of his work, and one can surmise that this is because it appears too speculative, too remote from the style of contemporary literary theory. Nonetheless, it composes one of the main threads linking together Blanchot's studies of literature. The idea of the work in *L'Espace littéraire*, and the various figures that it commands – the anteriority of the poem, the belonging of poet and reader to the poem – constitute a renewed exposition of the same essential premises.

The comparison with *La Part du feu* is significant, since it allow us to situate this idea of the work, to identify its rhetorical function. It shows that this idea of the work has its origins in a *critical* understanding, a claim to represent the modern idea of the poetic. Once this filiation is recognized, it also becomes possible to sketch out Blanchot's location within literary history, or at least the givens with which any such historical reading would have to engage. It could, for example, be argued that Blanchot's work responds to a certain 'metaphysical' moment in modern poetry, that it revives and even accomplishes a historical idea of a poetic absolute. The critical encounter between literary studies and Blanchot would be programmed in advance from the moment such an understanding was established. To such a 'metaphysics' of poetry, the more secular and objective style of contemporary criticism, prescribed by its place within the institutions of knowledge and research, would oppose a theoretically informed perspective on the literary as a determinate technical possibility in language, a social institution, a specific form of cultural work. Its task, then, would be to understand the historical motivations which, during a certain moment, led to poetry becoming the object of such extravagant claims.

An alternative to this prospect is what we seek here. To this end, it will be necessary first to show that Blanchot's idea of the work is animated by a thought which cannot be simply be identified and dispensed with under the names of 'metaphysics' or 'theology'. I will undertake this task with reference to *L'Espace littéraire*. The conception of the work is central to the more concerted and architectural composition that characterizes this volume, in comparison with the earlier collections.

I begin with the axiomatic definition of the work (*l'oeuvre*), which appears in the opening pages of the text:

> The work – the work of art, the literary work – is neither finished nor unfinished: it is. What it says is exclusively this: that it is – and nothing more. Beyond this, it is nothing. If one wants to make it express more, one will find nothing, one will find that it expresses nothing. (EL 14–15, 22)

The literariness of the work is concentrated in the fact that the work *is*. What this signifies is suggested by contrast with the ways in which the work is thereby *not* seen. The literary work is not to be seen as 'finished' or 'unfinished', and it is not to be seen as 'expressing' something *other* than the fact that it is. At the beginning of a later section, entitled 'The Characteristics of the Work of Art' (EL VII.ii), Blanchot writes:[1]

> The work does not immediately refer to someone who would have created it. When we know nothing of the circumstances which have prepared it, of the history of its creation, when we do not even know the name of the one who made it possible, then the work is closest to its own nature (*se rapproche le plus d'elle-même*). This is its true direction. (293, 221)

The work is 'closest to its own nature', when it is disconnected from all relations to the human world, including the act that brings it into being, and the work of understanding, by which it would it would enter into relation with the meaning and values of the reader. That the work 'says exclusively this – that it is, and nothing more' signifies, then, that it preserves a distance from all the relations in which it stands – the 'distance of the work from itself, from the reader, from the world, from other works' (268, 201).

This term – 'the work' – has terminological value in Blanchot, and by no means coincides with what one understands by 'the literary work' in normal usage. In order to approach the sense of the term here, it is essential to see that the 'being' of the work – its concentration into the fact of its presence – does not signify the stability of an identity, the self-sameness of the masterpiece, preserved in its immobility as human societies rise and fall around it (cf. EL 269, 202). The work, for Blanchot, is conceived as an *event*:

> That the work *is* marks the irruption, the radiance of a unique event, something which the understanding can subsequently

---

1 The sequence of these texts is not represented by their appearance in the volume, *L'Espace littéraire*. 'The Characteristics of the Work of Art' (EL VII.ii) is among the first written, appearing in May 1952, in *Les Temps modernes* (79). This is also by far the most explicitly Heideggerean, and it was still more so in its initial journal appearance: comparison of the two versions shows a clear movement to erase or at least reduce the Heideggerean language in the book version.

take hold, to which it feels it owes its beginning, but which it only grasps at first as eluding it [. . .] (EL 295, 222).

As 'event', the literary work is not something that is present and known: it 'does not belong with the assurance of stable truth, nor with the certainty of the familiar domain [. . .]' (Ibid). The 'work' is only present, Blanchot writes, in a second axiomatic passage from the beginning of the text, when the reader and the writer 'belong' to it and share in its 'solitude':

> The one who lives in the dependence of the work, whether in writing it or in reading it, belongs to the solitude of that which expresses only the word being – the word that language shelters in dissimulating it, or allows to appear in disappearing into the silent void of the work. [. . .] The work is solitary; this does not mean that it remains incommunicable, or that it lacks a reader. But the one who reads it enters into the affirmation of the solitude of the work, just as the one who writes it belongs to the risk of this solitude. [. . .]
>
> The writer writes a book, but the book is not yet the work, the work is only a work when the word being is pronounced through it, an event which is accomplished when the work is the immediate proximity (*l'intimité*) of someone who writes it and someone who reads it. (EL 15, 22–23)

Blanchot's poetics is shaped by an inner torsion: it is of the essence of the work that it takes place alone, that it is impersonal, separate from human meaning and from the human world, and yet it has this 'solitude' only in the reading and the writing, not in itself. What is added in *L'Espace littéraire* to the sketch of the work in *La Part du feu*, is the depiction of writing and reading, the 'solitude' that is proper to each, inasmuch as they belong to the work. The elaboration of this claim occupies much of the text, and it is in this sense that one can read the work as commanded by the initial definitions.

We will examine the conception of reading and writing that is here announced in some detail, since it forms the main axis of *L'Espace littéraire*, and in working out these claims, Blanchot advances his idea of the poetic, and also the guidelines for his criticism. But let us note first an element which is very significant for the relation of this thought to literary criticism. If the work is an event that is only accomplished in this proximity (at times referred to as 'communication', cf. EL VI.ii) of reading and writing, then it cannot be identified with the 'work' that is given to us by the library and the museum, by the institutions of culture and knowledge:

> The work is a thing among others, of use to men, and of interest to men: as such, it can become a means to an end, an object of knowledge, of culture and even of vanity. In this sense, the work has a history: men of learning and of taste can devote themselves to it, study it, write its history and the history of the art that the work represents. By the same token, however, the work in this sense is nothing but an object, which in the end only has value for the realizing will (*le souci réalisateur*), of which knowledge is merely one form.
>
> The work is not present, when it is merely the object of knowledge and interest, a product among other products. (EL 303, 228)

One should not overlook the 'extreme' quality of this position. The claim is that when criticism or literary history or indeed any kind of institutional and methodical enterprise deal with literary works, then the work is simply not present (cf. EL 274, 206, for an even more strident statement to this effect). Such a declaration does not altogether accurately reflect the relation of Blanchot's writing to knowledge and scholarship in general: many of the essays develop out of an engagement with scholarly works, and these responses are by no means simply polemical and antagonistic. Indeed, it is clear that his work – however idiosyncratic it may seem measured by academic criteria – depends, at the very least, upon the philological enterprise for the provision of the texts, and one can also think that it would not really be intelligible without at least something of the frame of reference given by literary scholarship.

It is not a matter of a polemical denigration of scholarship in favour of a supposed more immediate and spontaneous approach to literary works, but rather a questioning of the givenness of the literary work. There is some resemblance between such a reflection and movements in literary theory, such as reception theory and certain forms of historicism, which oppose the reading of texts as self-contained artefacts, arguing that the literary work only has its reality within a dynamic field of relations, only inasmuch as it is present to the real or virtual reader or audience, or inasmuch as it is mediated by the cultural institutions which grant value and social reality to art and literature. In the immediate context in which Blanchot is writing, there are marked similarities with Sartre's *Qu'est-ce que la littérature* (*What Is literature?*), published in 1948, which proposes a phenomenological analysis of the literary work. For Sartre also, the literary work only has its genuine reality within the space of its reading:

> To make [the work] come into view a concrete act called reading is necessary, and it lasts only as long as this can last. Otherwise, it is only black marks on paper. [. . .] The operation of writing implies that of reading as its dialectical correlative and these two connected acts necessitate two distinct agents. It is the joint effort of author and reader which brings upon the scene that concrete and imaginary object which is the work of the mind.[2]

Sartre's analysis can be differentiated from Blanchot's in that it is concerned with the literary work as a specific form of objectivity: the reading is a moment in the constitution of the literary object because our own works 'never seem to us *objective*' (49, Sartre's italics). The reading is part of the work because, through it, the work passes out of the subjective domain, out of the incompleteness adhering to anything that one has written oneself, and hence that one feels could still be improved, and attains the distance and independence of an object. For Blanchot, however, reading and writing are not moments in the constitution of an object, but in the 'being' of the work. This is more than a terminological difference: it points to what is most specific and difficult in Blanchot's conception of the work. When it is argued, in literary theory and aesthetics, that it is the reader who realizes the aesthetic dimension of the work, or that it is the institutions of culture which give social meaning

---

2   *What Is Literature?* Trans. Bernard Frechtman. London: Routledge, 2005, 50, and 51–52. Sartre underlines the consequence that the writer cannot read his own work (cf. 50), a thesis which Blanchot appropriates; cf. EL 17–18, 23–24, for Blanchot's version of this theme. For a study situating Sartre's work in the context of the poetics of Valéry and surrealism, and tracing the continuation of this line in the literary theories of the 1960s and 1970s, see Suzanne Guerlac, *Literary Polemics: Bataille, Sartre, Valéry, Breton*. Stanford: Stanford UP, 1997.

to words such as 'art' and 'literature', then the artwork is seen as a function of a constitutive process. For all such theories, the aesthetic experience is dependent upon the subjective and/or institutional instances that grant the work artistic status. Such claims are deeply alien to the orientation of Blanchot's discourse on art and literature, which would reverse this structure. The moments of human activity in the work – the act of creating the work and that of receiving the work – take their origin and their directives from the work itself, rather than determining it through an act of will and intelligence. We have seen this claim in *La Part du feu*: in modern poetry (in 'poets such as Mallarmé and Hölderlin", PF 254, 261), the poem claims to be anterior to reader and writer: reader and writer are only granted their existence by the work that precedes and contains them. This claim is only more pronounced in *L'Espace littéraire*, where it commands the description of the various dimensions of the poetic phenomenon. Thus it is the reader who allows the work to be – and yet this work of 'letting be' is anticipated by the work itself: 'it is the poem itself that affirms itself as a work in the reading, which engenders the reading that receives it, in the space held open by the reader' (EL 263, 198). Similarly, the poem is said to pre-exist the poet who 'only exists after the poem', who owes his 'reality' to the poem (EL 302, 227).

In order to engage with such claims, one needs first to clarify the terrain upon which they proceed. For this reason, before we turn to the details of Blanchot's poetics in *L'Espace littéraire*, I propose to sketch out certain elements of Heidegger's thought. For this thought, as we will see, holds the key, not only to the sense of this division of the work that we have been tracing, but also to much of what may otherwise appear as purely 'literary' in Blanchot's discourse.

II

The separation of 'the work', as the genuine artistic phenomenon, from the objective domain of knowledge parallels statements of Heidegger in 'The Origin of the Work of Art.' For Heidegger, when works of art are displayed in exhibitions, when canonical literary works are published in scholarly editions, the works themselves are not encountered. What is present then is rather the 'objects of the art business', 'the object of knowledge'. However professionally the work of scholarship and curatorship is performed, the works are torn out of the space proper to them (*aus ihrem eigenen Wesensraum*). The work in this more restrictive sense (*das Werksein des Werkes*) 'belongs solely in the space which it opens up itself'[3] The argument rests on a distinction, close to that which we have encountered in Blanchot, between the essence of art or poetry (*das Wesen der Kunst, das Wesen der Dichtung*), realized only when the work manifests itself within the space proper to it, and art as a form of cultural activity.[4]

The clarification of this point requires a recapitulation of certain elements of Heidegger's thought. It should be noted at the outset, however, that the discussion of Heidegger must be severely limited in the interest of our own concerns. For, as will soon become apparent, the question takes us directly into Heidegger's conception of 'man' or '*Dasein*', that is to say, into the centre of one of the most extensive, labyrinthine and complex of all modern philosophical works. But even a rapid indication of some moments in Heidegger's discourse can provide a frame of reference to approach the idea of 'the work' in Blanchot.

As a first orientation, one can say that Heidegger proposes that we consider the apparent division of the world between a totality of objects and a subject standing over opposed to it, knowing and acting upon it, as founded in a more original relation between the human (as *Dasein*) and being (*Sein*). Our discussions in earlier chapters permit us here to recall with great brevity the outlines of this thesis. Heidegger, we have seen, departs from the premise that whenever the human

---

3 *Holzwege* Frankfurt: Klostermann, 1976, 26–27. This conception of poetry aligns itself with the poetics of Hölderlin, upon which Heidegger's writings on art and poetry constantly draw. In a letter to his brother dated 1 January 1799 (and cited in the first of Heidegger's texts on poetry, 'Hölderlin and the Essence of Poetry') Hölderlin distinguishes between the undemanding outer aspect of art, its form and appearance of a game, and the power of art, when its true nature is present, to gather men together (Hölderlin, *Sämtliche Werke*, vol. 6, 1, 305). Similarly, in a letter to Christian Gottfried Schutz, in the context of a discussion of Greek art, a distinction is drawn between an 'outer' function of art, as diversion and pleasure, and its more essential nature, as a sacred dispensation, *eine heilige Schicklichkeit* (Hölderlin, *Sämtliche Werke*, vol.6, 1, 381).
4 Jacques Taminiaux shows that the main elements of this division between the reality and the mere objective existence of the work in Heidegger are already present in Hegel's *Aesthetics*; see 'The Hegelian Legacy in Heidegger's Overcoming of Aesthetics,' in *Poetry, Speculation and Judgment*. Trans. Michael Gendre. Albany, NY: SUNY Press, 1993, 127–152.

exists, beings in general, things and human selves are discovered and evident (*offenbar*). The discovery of beings – ontic truth – is only possible, however, inasmuch as it is anticipated by a prior understanding of being. 'Existence', in Heidegger, does not signify primarily the contingency and irreplaceability of the individual as mortal and historical (which is the basic meaning it has in 'existentialism'). The force of the term is rather to underline that existence, as finite and historical, 'stands in the clearing of being'[5] . This initial 'clearing' (*Lichtung*) in which and thanks to which we encounter all that 'is' cannot, however, be considered as a *property* of man, in the sense of a permanent characteristic (as is, for example, the transcendental dimension in Kant). The 'open' (*das Offene*), as Heidegger says in the essay on the artwork, is not like an empty stage on which we enter and exit: 'the unconcealment of beings is never merely an ongoing condition, but rather it is something that happens (or an event, *ein Geschehen, ein Geschehnis*)' (*Holzwege* 41). Through its event character, the light of being is inextricably linked to human existence, dependent upon human participation in order to take place, and hence marked by the element of decision and contingency in which the human lives.

The idea of truth as unconcealment implies at the same time a modification in the understanding of the human. In place of the closed autonomy of the 'subject' – that is to say, in place of a conception of the human for which the primary given is the cognitive and technical–instrumental relation to an objective world – man now appears as the site that is required in order for being to open up and to prevail. With this specification is entailed a distinct sphere of human accomplishment, incomparable to all other spheres. This accomplishment, in its factical reference, however, can be variously located and conceived. In *Sein und Zeit*, the understanding of being is located at the level of the *individual* existence, with the self which has inalienably to be itself, and which exists in view of its mortality. The formal designation of the human as 'being-in-the-world' signifies that the opening up of the world – the disclosure of being as such, the 'there' in being-there (*Dasein*) – takes place in and through the advent of human existence. Prior to any specific relation, any limitation or possibility that marks

---

5 'Letter on Humanism' in *Pathmarks*. Ed. William McNeil. Cambridge: Cambridge UP, 1998, 247.

the human by its situation *in* the world, human existence 'lets world happen'. The existence of the human has an event character. With the advent of the human, the world breaks into entities, lighting them and allowing them to have the being that they cannot have otherwise than in a world (*Pathmarks*, 122–123).

This conception is worked out from different angles and recast by Heidegger in most of the main texts of the 1930s. In 'On the Essence of Truth', the space within which beings can appear is termed 'the open': the open is 'opened' and 'preserved' by the advent of freedom, defined as the movement by which the human lets itself into the open (*sich auf das Offene einlassen*). The transformation in the terminology is less important in this context than the shift in the frame of reference. In the earlier work, the 'event' of this opening is located at the level of the individual existence – that is, of each existence in its singularity – in its struggle to be itself, to 'win' itself, in the terms of the existential dilemma articulated through the alternative of authenticity and inauthenticity in *Sein und Zeit*. Now it comes to be identified with an historical event in the domain of thought and in language. The discussion of freedom, in 'On the Essence of Truth', for example, does not make any remarks about individual freedom at all. Instead, the explication is made concrete by reference to the initial questioning of the nature of being in ancient Greek philosophy.

The shift from the fundamental–ontological horizon of *Sein and Zeit*, in which the exposition is centred around the structures of being-in-the world, to the philosophical–historical horizon of Heidegger's later work, concerned with the history of being (*Seinsgeschichte*), results in a more prominent place being given to poetry and art. As the pre-eminent Heidegger scholar, Friedrich von Herrmann writes: 'Technology, politics and art emerge as topics for the first time in Heidegger's thinking only with the turn from fundamental ontology, as the first elaboration of the question of being, to the second elaboration of this question in the perspective of the history of being'.[6] In the texts of the 1930s, the accomplishment of transcendence, the formation of world, is presented as taking place in a series of dimensions of thought and praxis,

---

6 *Martin Heidegger: Politics, Art and Technology*. Ed. Karsten Harries and Christoph Jammes, NY: Holmes and Meier, 1994, 55.

including art and poetry as well as philosophy (and also, problematically, statesmanship and the political). I will consider this development here by briefly examining two texts from this period: first the essay, 'On the Origin of the Work of Art' (first delivered as a lecture and then passing through two significant revisions to reach its final form in 1936) and then the lecture course, *Introduction to Metaphysics*, delivered in 1935, but not published until 1953 (when it was the first of Heidegger's lecture courses to have been published).

The essay 'On the Origin of the Work of Art' begins by questioning the interpretive framework and the categories through which the artwork tends to be understood. Our thought about art has been guided, Heidegger suggests, by the opposition of form and matter, 'the conceptual schema for all aesthetics and art theory' (*Holzwege* 12). The ontological horizon of aesthetics has therefore been shaped in an unreflected way by the model of the produced thing, and specifically, by the model of the thing of use, the tool, in which the 'matter' – the materials from which the tool is made – is submitted to the 'form' given by the idea, the purpose for which it is made. The opposition of form and content, derived from the sphere of things of use, has been taken over – with Plato, for Heidegger – as 'the immediately intelligible constitution of all beings' (14). Accordingly, the philosophical understanding of the work of art has taken the act of a forming consciousness at work on given materials as its implicit paradigm. But it is possible to question whether the artwork should be understood as a certain kind of artefact, as something like a thing of use with its usefulness suspended, as Heidegger sarcastically puts it. It is precisely this assumption that Blanchot opposes, we recall, in separating the literary from its mundane existence as 'a product among products' (EL 303, 228).

The question here, it must be underlined, is not whether the artwork is in fact produced by human work, but whether the fact and the process of its production defines the horizon from which it is to be thought. For Heidegger, 'the essence of art' is to be grasped with reference, not to the work that goes into it, and by which it is placed in the same horizon as all the things of the human world, but rather with reference to the work that it *performs* – the work of transcendence, by which the human gives itself a world. This claim is made through developments of great verbal complexity: the exposition is even more deeply rooted than usual in the resources of the German language,

Myth and Representation in Blanchot's Criticism   115

and cannot be studied in detail here.[7] It will suffice merely to recall the sequence of formulations through which the essay crystallizes its thought. The essence of art (*das Wesen der Kunst*) consists in the setting into work of the truth (*Holzwege* 21–25). This takes place in the work, the being of which consists in two primary traits: first, that it sets up a world, or that it holds open the open of the world (28–31), and second, that it is the pro-duction (*her-stellen*, in the sense of the setting forth, into the world) of 'the earth' (31–32). The work is 'the intimacy of the conflict' (*Innigkeit des Streites*) (36) between these two traits, the setting up of world, and the setting forth of earth: 'the being of the work consists in the enactment of the conflict between world and earth' (36). In enacting this conflict, the work of art is the 'happening of truth' (45), the inauguration of the open within which all things can be assigned the being that is proper to them. For truth to take place, for the light of being to be inaugurated, there has to be an entity, a being, in which the conflict of the opening and the concealment – the original conflict in truth itself, decided in the conflict between world and earth – can take form and be enacted. The artwork can be such an entity, but only inasmuch as it enters into its being *as* a work, into what Heidegger calls its 'pure standing in itself' (*das reine Insichstehen des Werkes*, 25). This character of the work is most fully realized, Heidegger suggests, when the createdness of the work is concentrated purely in the fact that it is (52–54). In order to realize this possibility, the artwork demands the effacement of the link to the artist and to the process of its production: for with this fact that the work 'is', we are opened on to the 'extraordinary', the wonder of wonders, that beings are (54), an event that exceeds the productive powers of any individual.

One sees, then, the substantial agreement between the doctrine of the work (*l'oeuvre*) in *L'Espace littéraire* and Heidegger's essay. In both cases, the properly artistic quality of the artwork, the poetic quality of the poem, lies in its pure 'being'. Furthermore, the work of art can only *be* – in the active sense of an event that is also the event or the

---

7   There are a number of good close analyses of this famous essay available in English. See, for example, William McNeil's discussion in his study, *The Glance of the Eye: Heidegger, Aristotle and the Ends of Theory*. Albany: SUNY Press, 1999. Again, the definitive study is Friedrich Wilhelm von Herrmann's book-length analysis, *Heideggers Philosophie der Kunst: eine systematische Interpretation der Holzwege-Abhandlung 'Der Ursprung des Kunstwerks'*, Frankfurt: Klostermann, 1980.

advent of truth – if it is *allowed* to be. This means that the reader or the viewer is a necessary moment in the realization of the work, no less than the writer or artist. The reader or spectator is, in Heidegger, the 'preserver', *der Bewahrer*, in which, by a play on the word (*be-wahren*), one has to hear also 'the one who makes the work true', the one who gives to it the truth that happens with it. More important even than these verbal and structural similarities is the guidance Heidegger's essay can give us in understanding the horizon of Blanchot's poetics. Heidegger's discourse does not have its primary frame of reference in the experience of actual works of art, actual poems and novels. In determining the work of art as the 'happening of truth', 'the conflict of world and earth', Heidegger is not giving a 'poetic' re-description of the work that we know and experience, in the classroom or in the circulation of culture. In the *Introduction to Metaphysics*, he writes of the necessity 'to give a new content to the word "art" and to what it names on the basis of a renewed and authentic basic position with regard to being', and the essay on the work of art can be seen as his attempt to realize this proposal.[8] It would not, however, be accurate to say that ontology merely dictates a concept of art, in the sense of a consequence derived from an a priori given. Certainly, for Heidegger, the question of being is the first among questions (as he argues in the opening pages of the *Introduction to Metaphysics*). But the thought of being is not then simply 'applied' to various ontic regions. In accord with the 'circularity' which he had identified as the burden of all genuine thought in *Being and Time*, the thought of being, the horizon for the understanding of art, is worked out in and through the presentation of the phenomenon (just as it is, in many other texts, it is worked out in the course of the engagement with the texts of the philosophical tradition). For Heidegger, moreover, this is also the case, though in an unacknowledged way, in any science, or indeed in any discourse, which will always reproduce the ontological foundations (e.g. the understanding of the world in terms of the subject) on which it stands, along with the positive determinations it seeks to establish.

In recognizing this point, one can avoid certain pitfalls in reading Blanchot: it is not so much the thought itself that is the same, but the separation from a representational inquiry, such as literary criticism

---

8   *Einführung in die Metaphysik*. Tübingen: Niemeyer, 1998, 101.

and literary theory, that takes the givenness of the work of art to the inquiring subject, for granted. This is precisely the reason why the terminology and the rhetoric of Blanchot's texts are so alien to the language of literary studies, and why there is bound to be a distortion in any 'translation' of Blanchot's work into the schemes of literary study.

We can take some guidance in reading Blanchot's poetics from the *Introduction to Metaphysics*. There are passages in *L'Espace littéraire*, which echo both this text and the essay on the work of art.[9] My concern, however, is not to document sources, but to draw out certain basic assumptions which are stated more clearly in Heidegger than in Blanchot, who gives only the most minimal indications as to his method and assumptions, and most often none at all. The central parts of the *Introduction to Metaphysics* are occupied with the reading of the pre-Socratics (and Sophocles), and is concerned in particular with the meaning of certain key words: *physis, alētheia, tekhnē, legein, noein* among others. The purpose of the reading is not ultimately to propose an understanding the Greek authors for their own sake, but rather, through the study of these texts, to reawaken the experience of being that, for Heidegger, constitutes the element of Greek thought, although it was never thought as such by the Greeks themselves.[10] The dominance of the experience of being in which we now move is apparent in the difficulty of reading these texts, and the systematic distortion that modern thought places upon them. In order to approach them, we have to suspend the familiar schema of subjective activity (*Einführung*, 104). The separation from the element of subjectivity is more here than an interpretive precaution: in a sense, what the pre-Socratics offer is precisely the invitation to hear words such as language, thought or art in a way other than we tend to – no longer to understand these terms as a faculty, a way of acting, proper to the human, under the guidance of an idea of the human that is taken

---

9 For example, the reference to the 'strangeness and the excess of being' (*l'étrangeté et la démesure de l'être'*, EL 237, 179) seems very close to the (now well-known) discussion of man as the strangest and most excessive being in the chorus from *Antigone* in Heidegger's lectures.
10 'Authentic interpretation has to show that which is not actually said in the words of the text, and yet nonetheless is said' (*Einführung*, 124). On the contrast between the Greek experience and the Greek thought, see *Vorträge und Aufsätze*. Pfullingen: Günther Neske, 1954, 220–221.

over from the discourses of biology, psychology and epistemology (107). Rather than understanding such words as attributes or abilities attached to an idea of the human which is already given – which, for Heidegger, is what takes place in the famous definition of man as the animal that can speak – the reading of these texts invite us to proceed in the opposite direction, and to understand the human on the basis of a renewed understanding of language (or art). What is named as *legein* (in Heraclitus), *noein* (in Parmenides) and *tekhnē* (in Sophocles) is a possibility of belonging to being (here thought as *physis* and as *logos*), of 'taking place' with it.[11] 'Belonging' here expresses a modality that equates neither to a subjective act, nor to a simple ontological inclusion, given from the beginning; it is, rather, the response to the appeal that comes from being itself, a response that is accomplished in turning away from absorption in and dominance by beings. The 'essence of the human' is to be determined in terms of this possibility, which does not proceed from our will, but is rather an event that possesses us, and makes us who we are.[12]

We see that what is said here about language or art (*tekhnē*) by way of the exegesis of the Greek texts is not a *theoretical* concept, a definition that would circumscribe language or thinking, such as we encounter them in self-reflection or at large in the world. The descriptive–cognitive model of what is simply there (*die Beschreibung und die Feststellung eines Vorhandenen*, 114) is refused the primary validity for an approach to the phenomena in question. The alternative approach that is opened up is not directed towards any kind of knowledge or theory. What Heidegger refers to as the projection of a poetic thinking (*ein dichterische-denkenden Entwurf*) does not ask the question of each phenomenon in isolation: in thinking the phenomenon, it is always also determining its horizon in an understanding of the self and world – a process which, for Heidegger, has to pass by way of the question of being.

---

11 '*Vernehmung ist nicht eine Verhaltungsweise, die der Mensch als Eigenschaft hat, sondern umgekehrt: Vernehmung ist jenes Geschehnis, das den Menschen hat*' (108).

12 '*Wir mussen erfahren lernen, das sich erst aus dem Geschehnis der Wesenszugehörigkeit von Sein und Vernehmung das Sein des Menschen bestimmt*' (107). The work of art, for Heidegger, no less than the work of thought, is this event (*Geschehnis*): as such it is anterior to the one that creates it, since the work is not the product of someone or some group who already exists and has certain known quantities; rather the creator (and the one who preserves it in responding to it, *der Bewahrer*) comes to be, as a result of the work.

III

Let us now return to Blanchot. I will begin with a brief text in which many of the rhetorical and narrative structures of *L'Espace littéraire* come together. The text is without title and appears at the beginning of Section II of *L'Espace littéraire*, entitled 'Approach to the Literary Space'. It begins:

> The poem – literature – seems to be linked to a speech (*une parole*) which cannot be interrupted because it does not speak: it is. The poem is not this speech itself, for the poem is a beginning, whereas this speech never begins, but always speaks again, always recommences. However, the poet is the one who has heard this speech, who has made himself into the hearing of it, (*qui s'en est fait l'entente*), the mediator who has imposed silence upon it by pronouncing it. In this speech, the poem is close to the origin, for all that is original is exposed to this pure un-power of repetition, the sterile prolixity, the excess of that which can do nothing, of that which is never the work, which ruins the work and restores inertia without end (*le désoeuvrement sans fin*). This is a source perhaps, but it is a source which must, in a certain manner, be made to cease in order to become a resource. [. . .]
>
> [The poet] has heard the interminable, the incessant, as language (*comme parole*), has attuned himself to it (*est entré dans son entente*), has held himself in its demand, and lost himself in it, and yet, having sustained it, he has necessarily made it cease, and in this intermittence, he has rendered it apprehensible (*saisissable*), has preferred it by firmly reconciling it with this limit. He has mastered it by imposing measure. (EL 35–36, 37)[13]

---

13 'Une parole' can signify 'word' in the sense of a significant utterance, a sense that is stronger in the German *Wort*. This is the translation given by Smock, for which there is something to be said; this is surely the sense of 'parole' in the title of the text 'La Parole sacrée de Hölderlin', (cf. our Chapter 2), for example. But I take *parole* here in the sense of speech or even language, since this seems to be the direction of the variant terms used to designate the same phenomenon: 'the language that no-one speaks' (*langage que personne ne parle*), 'the speech (*la parole*) of the original experience', 'a voice without words' (EL, 21, 58, 302: 26, 53, 226). On this motif in Blanchot, see Chapter 3 of Anne-Lise Schulte Nordholt, *Maurice Blanchot: l'écriture comme experience du dehors*. Geneva: Droz, 1995.

120 Blanchot and Literary Criticism

The depiction of the poet as 'the mediator', entering into proximity to the language of origin, belonging to it and silencing it, is one among several mythic sequences in *L'Espace littéraire*: others include the representation of the poetic condition as exile (EL III) or as belonging to 'the night' (EL V.iii), the rewriting of the myth of Orpheus (EL V.ii), and the appropriation of elements of Hölderlin's representation of the poetic vocation (EL VII, tacitly present here in the reference to the poet as the 'mediator', cf. our Chapter 2).[14] The parallels and echoes between these sequences generate the constant verbal resonance characteristic of Blanchot's writing. But each motif is also developed for its own sake, often gathering density and meaning through a sequence of repetitions. Such is the case with the figure of the poet as the hearing of this 'neutral' speech, which becomes the topic of intense development during a brief period of Blanchot's production, and then reappears periodically, though usually more briefly, in later texts. The main texts, all either collected in *L'Espace littéraire*, or written during the same period include: 'The Work and the Erring Speech' (originally published together with the text on Kafka which immediately follows it in its book form, March 1952), 'Literature and the Original Experience' (May 1952), 'The Experience of Mallarmé', (July 1952), 'The Essential Solitude' (January, 1953), 'Inspiration, Lack of Inspiration,' (February–March, 1953) 'The Beast of Lascaux' (April 1953), and 'Where Now, Who Now' (October, 1953, on Beckett, collected in LV IV.iii).[15] In most of these texts, the elaboration of the mythic representation takes place in communication with a 'representational' discourse, concerned with real literary writers and works. In 'Inspiration, Lack of Inspiration', for example, this experience – now as the awareness of 'an infinite murmur, open by our side, beneath our everyday language' (239, 181), a 'neutral, indistinct language, which is the being of language' (240, 181) – is presented as the genuine content of the traditional notion of poetic inspiration, and

---

14 On this aspect of Blanchot's work, see 'Mythic Portrayals of Writing and Reading', in John Gregg, *Maurice Blanchot and the Literature of Transgression*. Princeton: Princeton UP, 1994, Chapter 4, 46–71.

15 The figuration of this sequence first appears, however, in the fictional text, *Au Moment voulu*, published in 1951. A brief text accompanying the work with its initial publication reproduces the language of this sequence, in order to formulate the ambition of this fiction. It is reproduced in Maurice Blanchot, *La Condition critique*. Ed. Christophe Bident. Gallimard, 2010, 189.

anticipations of it are discovered in a number of sources, including texts by Hofmannstahl, Keats, Kafka and Breton. Any reading of these texts, then, has to confront the question of the articulation between the mythic narrative and the critical claim to understanding.

The first step in response to this problem, I would suggest, is to recognize that this 'mythic' discourse condenses and mobilizes the thought that Blanchot develops elsewhere in a form closer to philosophical exposition. I have studied this thought in the preceding chapter, and I resume it here briefly, referring to 'Literature and the Right to Death'. 'When I speak, death speaks in me', Blanchot writes (PF 313, 323). The occupation of a world articulated by means of language supposes a relation to death that precedes all relation to what is merely present. When we name and make sense of the world in language, then death is a power, giving us things in their absence, inviting us to envisage and effect their transformation in view of our greater mastery; but in putting death to work, we have entered into a relation with 'the genius of absolute death' (*le génie de la mort absolue*) (PF 255, 263), with death as a power that is greater than our ability to anticipate and mobilize it. It is this power that the poet 'hears' in the 'infinite murmur' – a language behind language which cannot be silent, because in it 'silence speaks' (EL 56, 51). A 'pure un-power of repetition', a 'sterile prolixity', 'inertia without end', such is the aspect that language assumes when one hears in it, not the things that humans have sought to name, but the absence of things that is needed for naming to become possible.

The 'mythic' narratives have the function of representing reading and writing, on the basis of this understanding of language. Throughout the exposition of this sequence, the mythic and dramatic presentation of writing is proposed in place of existing conceptions of the literary activity. Writing is not a matter of expressing oneself with superior resources, with greater than usual talent, with a heightened consciousness and memory, with a sense for the musicality of language: it is the approach to this point where language is not yet language, where language is imaginary, the murmur of the incessant and the interminable (EL 51–56, 46–52). In its negative face, the text is in communication with existing discourse on literature and art; in its positive face, it seems to inhabit a discursive space entirely apart. It is in order to measure and conceptualize this separation that we have had recourse to Heidegger's work. The construction of a mythic and narrative space of writing has the same function as Heidegger's work of translation and interpretation from the Greeks: it revises the philosophical foundations that are always implicitly present, when we speak of language, thought, or writing. Certain elements of Blanchot's text have close affinities with the texts from Heidegger considered here. The choice of the figure of the voice or the inarticulate speech to signify the presence of death in language is very close to a figure used by Heidegger in many of his later texts. In the postscript to *What Is Metaphysics?*, a text in which Heidegger restates his position during the 1940s, for example, he writes of the 'silent voice of being' and refers to philosophical thinking as the 'echo' of being.[16] But there are also more subtle affinities. In place of the language of making and doing, characteristic of art theory and poetics (creation, fiction, composition), Blanchot deploys a series of similar verbal phrases to designate the act of writing. Writing is a hearing (*entendre, se faire l'entente*), an enduring (*soutenir*), a belonging (*appartenir*), a holding oneself in (*se tenir dans*), a maintaining of a contact, an approach (often *une approche de* ... with an ambiguity as to whether the writer is approaching or being approached), at the limit, a losing of oneself (*se perdre*). The use of verbs such as 'belonging' and 'hearing' in this series points towards Heidegger's thought, since these words translate terms that play an important role in Heidegger's texts.[17] We have seen that for Heidegger, the relation to being is not a given, but something that is 'accomplished' by the human (*Dasein*), enacted in art and thought; through the reinterpretation of the key words of Greek thought, Heidegger elaborates a language in order to express the understanding that this accomplishment is not the causing of an effect, but the response to an appeal, to the claim that is made upon thought by being.[18]

---

16 *Pathmarks*, 236. Georgio Agamben, in the course of an original configuration of the relations of language, death and being, argues that the silent voice is the constant figure for being in the Western tradition: *Language and Death: The Place of Negativity*. Trans. Karen E. Pinkus. Minneapolis: University of Minnesota Press, 1991.
17 On the connection between belonging (*gehören*) and hearing (*hören*), see the essay 'Logos' in *Vorträge und Aufsätze*, 205–209.
18 Compare the opening statement of the 'Letter on Humanism', questioning the dominant subject-based conception of activity (*Handeln*) as the bringing about of an effect, and sketching out an alternative interpretation of the relations of acting, thinking, the human, language and being (*Pathmarks* 239).

It is along the same lines, I would suggest, that one should read the dramatization of the poetic act as the 'hearing' of the 'incessant speech' in *L'Espace littéraire*. The positive sense that is given to the poem by Blanchot concerns the work that it accomplishes, rather than the properties of an artefact – the creation of a silence, the granting of a beginning. Blanchot's discourse is not, then, oriented towards the definition of poetry or writing as a particular kind of entity or activity within the world, marking its separation from non-poetic and almost poetic forms of language. It is not a question of the definition of art, but of the possibility that art and poetry represent – the realization of a relation to the initial absence, that is given with language. The silence that the poem creates comes from the proximity in which it stands, through the poet, to the sterile prolixity, the beginning from the contact that the poet maintains with the language that never begins, *le désoeuvrement sans fin*.

The challenge of this conception and the verbal complexities to which it gives rise come in part from the need to conceive 'possibility' or 'accomplishment' in a sense that is not that of the action involved in knowing and transforming the world. Blanchot presents the 'work' or the 'poem' as something in which the writer participates, rather than something that he produces or creates. One of the main ways in which this idea is proposed in *L'Espace littéraire* is through the thesis that the event of the work is never in the dependence of an individual existence, and has its 'being' only from the participation of the reader. Still within the brief text that we have been reading, this is stated as follows:

> The poet – the one who writes, the 'creator' – could never express the work from out of the essential inertia. Never could he, by himself, cause the pure language of beginning to spring forth from what is at the origin. That is why the work is a work only when it becomes the inner space shared by someone who writes and someone who reads, the space violently opened by the contestation between the power to speak and the power to hear.
> (*Jamais le poète, celui qui écrit, le 'créateur', ne pourrait du désoeuvrement essentiel exprimer l'oeuvre; jamais à lui seul, de ce qui est à l'origine, faire jaillir la pure parole du commencement. C'est pourquoi, l'oeuvre est oeuvre seulement quand elle devient l'intimité ouverte de quelqu'un qui l'écrit et de quelqu'un qui la lit, l'espace*

violemment déployé par la contestation mutuelle du pouvoir de dire et du pouvoir d'entendre). (35, 37)

The work only *is* when reading and writing inhabit and contest the space opened by the work. If their relation unfolds as the violence of a contestation, it is because the work itself is the tension of a conflict. The figure of the work as the enactment of a conflict is another motif that is presented and restated in a number of the texts of the period. It makes its first appearance in a text on René Char, published in 1946 and then collected in *La Part du feu*, and then becomes the object of a more intensive elaboration in a sequence of texts, including 'The Characteristics of the Work of Art' (first appearing in May 1952, then as EL VII.ii), 'The Beast of Lascaux' (April 1953, but not collected until the later collection, *Une Voix venue d'ailleurs*) and above all 'Communication' (December 1953), which proposes something like a formal synthesis of what has been developed with regard to reading, writing and the work in *L'Espace littéraire*. It is to this last essay that I will here refer.

The text begins with the affirmation that reading in the true sense, in the 'literary' sense, is not the capacity of someone who knows how to read, and who reads one work after another. The reader, like the writer, has to belong to the work: the reading is nothing but the consent that allows the work to 'be'; the sole act of the reader (*le lecteur*) is to open the space in which the work gives rise to the reading (*la lecture*), indeed, makes itself into the reading, or more precisely, makes itself into the 'communication' between the moments of power and impossibility, represented by reader and writer:

> The communication of the work does not lie in the fact that it has become communicable, through reading, to a reader. The work is itself communication, the proximity and the conflict between the demand of reading and the demand of writing, between the measure of the work which becomes power and the excess (*démesure*) of the work which tends to impossibility, between the form in which it gives itself and the absence of limit in which it refuses itself, between the decision which it is as commencement and the indecision that it is as recommencement. (EL 263, 199)

The work for Blanchot is only ever its genesis, the movement from impossibility to presence, (cf. EL 265–267, 199–201): it is never a result, never the end point of a real labour – its existence as such a 'product' is what Blanchot terms the 'book', the work as known and appreciated in the element of scholarship and culture. The work is dependent for its existence upon the reader and writer, who enact the conflict between its moments. We are invited to understand, however, that this conflict, in which the work has its life and reality, is only apparently the struggle of two powers, existing separately as reader and writer, each with the will to shape and possess the work. The work precedes reader and writer, granting each their sense and very existence; this essential thesis is preserved from the texts of *La Part du feu*, with which we began. The relationship between reader and writer is merely the final form assumed by a conflict internal to the work – 'a more original struggle between less distinct demands, inseparable and irreconcilable, demands that we call measure and excess, form and infinity, decision and indecision, and which under their successive oppositions tend to give reality to the same violence' (264, 199). The struggle, the text proceeds to indicate, is at its origin, the movement by which, through the work, the 'obscure' comes to light, by which 'dissimulation appears' (265, 199) – or in the terms of the figure that we have studied here (of which the rhetoric of 'the obscure' is merely a parallel variation) – by which the work marks a beginning, in the silence that it imposes upon 'the incessant, the interminable' (35–36, 37).

Reading and writing, then, belong together as two moments of one event (in the sense of the Heideggerean *Geschehen*): they constitute the space – the open proximity (*intimité ouverte*, 35, 37) – within which the conflict that makes up the being of the work is enacted. As such, each exists only by virtue of its tension with the other, and each can transform into its opposite. The moment of reading is foreshadowed within writing, as the point at which writing tears itself away from impossibility (265, 199). Conversely, the power and the 'lightness' that Blanchot associates with reading, in contrast to the infinite labours of writing, can end by being absorbed back into the genesis of the work, and rejoin the experience of the writer (cf. 269–270, 202–203).

The descriptions of writing and reading that occupy much of *L'Espace littéraire* show how the demand of the work (*l'exigence de l'oeuvre*) appears within the factical experiences of literary reading and literary writing, transforming these 'activities' from within, making them something other than a form of power at the disposal of the reader and writer, as individuals in the world. For the writer, the attunement of his language to the 'infinite murmur' beneath language erodes his words, makes them into the mere image of words, affecting them with an inertia and a passivity that makes writing impossible. For the reader, on the contrary, the proximity of language in the work to its origin means that the work has the force of 'beginning' (*commencement*). Reading, too, demands a leap back to the space at which 'nothing yet has meaning' (258, 196) – and yet this experience is not one of anxiety or despair, but of 'happiness' and 'innocence' (261, 197); it is 'the revelation of the unique, inevitable unpredictable work' (260, 197).

The pattern of contrast that organizes the presentation of reading and writing does not exclude the presence of deeper common traits. In their engagement with the work, both reader and the writer are presented as essentially impersonal. The demand (*exigence*) to which each is subject consists in a separation from the self, from the particular, empirical self no less than from the general self of knowledge. In the case of writing, this separation is experienced as a burden and a privation, whereas, for the reading, it offers rather a freedom from the self. The writer becomes 'no one', becomes the 'he', rather than the 'I' (EL 23, 26–27). The reader, on the other hand, abandons the weight of his acquired knowledge and preconceptions, and attains to the light, impersonal presence that does nothing more than allow the work to be (EL 255, 193–194). In each case the demand that defines them separates them from the experience of the world as organized by *work*, by the structure of the project, of means directed towards an end. Writing exceeds the frame of work, it is a work deprived of a possible end, extending into infinity (cf. LV 130–131, 93–94). Reading, on the other hand, lies this side of work: it is nothing more than a movement of consent, the acceptance of a gift (EL 258–259, 196). Both have in common, therefore, that they occupy a time that is distinct from that of development and becoming. Writing has no present: it never commences, but rather finds itself in the midst of an indefinite repetition which cannot acquire the force of an event. Reading has only the pure present, the now of the first time, the beginning announced by the work.

IV

One can readily foresee the opposition that this remarkable construction would encounter from the literary–critical establishment. The complexity and the multiplicity of real poetry, real works of art, it will be objected, are here reduced back to an *a priori* schema whose origins are purely conceptual. Heidegger's presentation of the work as the conflict of world and earth – to which the conflict within the work that Blanchot describes is evidently close – is liable to the same critique.[19] In a sense, however, this kind of objection has already been anticipated, since we have underlined that what is proposed here is not a *theory* that would describe the reality of the poetry and the art that we know, but rather an intervention at the level of the basic concepts by which we encounter such works. It is altogether to be expected that such an understanding should be schematic, since it claims to sketch out in advance the essential relations supposed in the intelligibility of the 'thing'. The same simplicity is also present in the notion of 'literary creation' – as a current basic concept that commands most spontaneous discussion of literary works – by which we understand the literary work as the result of the exercise of a shaping will upon the material of experience and language.

At the same time, however, one has to note that there is in fact a great deal about the realities of literary works in Blanchot. Where Heidegger's essay on 'The Origin of the Work of Art' is avowedly philosophical and contains nothing more than 'indications' (*Holzwege* 73) on art theory and criticism, *L'Espace littéraire* is much closer to what one normally understands by literary criticism. In order to assess Blanchot's contribution at this level, one has to consider the decisive

---

19 On the relation of Heidegger to literary studies, an excellent and too-little-known work is Jörg Appelhans, *Heideggers Ungeschriebene Poetologie*. Tübingen: Niemayer, 2002. This study is very aware of contemporary critical and theoretical debates in the U.S. which, rather than German literary criticism, is the main frame of reference. Although almost entirely negative in its conclusions as to the validity of Heidegger's analyses as readings, it examines the relation to criticism and method in all of Heidegger's writings on literature with great thoroughness, and assembles a veritable compendium of all possible critiques, the majority of which would also apply to Blanchot (which is not to imply that the situation in relation to study is simply the same in each case).

gesture by which the question of 'the origin of the work' (derived in part from Heidegger) is articulated with a discourse on the literary phenomenon, in the facticity, the detail and the complexity of its worldly existence.

For Blanchot, as we have seen, reading, in the proper sense of the term, is absorbed in the presence of the work: it is not a generally applicable aptitude, and certainly not a method. But Blanchot's own essays often do not appear to put this principle into practice. It can readily be shown that Blanchot's critical studies propose a *general* understanding, rather than granting the pure priority of the work that he demands of the literary reading in his poetics. The claim to understanding is in fact very characteristic of his writings: phrases such as 'thus we understand' (*'on comprend pourquoi'*, *'c'est pourquoi'*) scan the texts. In *L'Espace littéraire* and *Le Livre à venir*, Blanchot often describes a specific predicament encountered by 'the writer', generating a number of possible paths that can be taken. The pattern is proposed in the form of brief sketches and narratives of writing, drawing on literary tradition or apocrypha (biography, anecdote), as well as through the interpretations of myths (Orpheus, the Sirens), and the discussion of specific literary works. There is no attempt to establish the legitimacy of this mode of analysis, or to stipulate any kind of limits to its deployment, above all with regard to the way in which the analyses are reproduced at multiple levels, textual, biographical and mythic. But there is an unmistakable sense of an underlying consistency in these texts: terms such as 'solitude', 'fascination', or 'error' function in a manner that is not far removed from the categories of an analysis that proceeds methodically in the interest of a developing cognition.

In 'The Essential Solitude' (EL I), this procedure is applied at the most pragmatic level, in discussing some of the typical difficulties encountered by writers. The writer 'never knows if he has finished his work'; he 'can never read his work', can never have it present, outside himself (14–18, 22–24). Literary writing, therefore, has a tendency to become an infinite labour: 'the solitude which comes to the writer by way of the work shows itself in this: writing is now the interminable, the incessant' (20, 26). At one level, these remarks have the air of empirical observations, generalizations from the data of literary diaries and biography. But they tend unmistakably towards a claim to see in such material the signs of an experience of a more general form. The distinctive experiential categories developed in *L'Espace littéraire* – essential solitude, *désoeuvrement*, fascination of the absence of time – have precisely this function: they allow the analyst to see what is at work in the peripeties of the creative process, beyond what is immediately accessible to the conscious self.

These claims, it is true, only refer to 'the writer', a designation which leaves the cognitive claim suspended in apparent fictionality. In fact, however, nearly all of what is developed in such passages corresponds to real episodes discussed in many other texts of this period. This content is often confined to mere allusions, sometimes brief portraits or sketches. In 'The Work and the Erring Speech', for example, Blanchot recalls Rimbaud's abandonment of poetry in the search for money and adventure, suggesting that this path was taken in order to help him to forget what the experience has opened up to him (EL 58, 53). In 'Inspiration', Blanchot reflects upon Van Gogh's self-mutilation, and in 'The Possible Death', the conduct of Nerval and Kleist in the time leading up to their suicides, illustrates the passivity of the self entering into the space of death (EL 127, 102). In other texts, there are evocations of Proust, the former socialite closeting himself away from all his friends, endlessly writing, rewriting (LV 284, 208); of Cézanne painting compulsively, dying with the brush in his hand, unable to even spare a day to attend his mother's funeral (LV 46, 31). Such passages may at times give the impression of being merely illustrative vignettes, primarily rhetorical in their intent. If one looks at the essays of this period as a whole, however, one sees that there is a specific hermeneutic procedure at work. One sees this, above all, in the texts on Kafka, the most sustained and detailed of the 'case studies'. In 1981, Blanchot published *De Kafka à Kafka*, collecting essays on Kafka from a period of over 20 years (though all the texts had already been published in previous collections). In reading this collection, one notes, firstly, that the reflection upon the literary experience really only begins at the moment of *L'Espace littéraire*. The essay 'Kafka and the Demand of the Work' (EL III.ii) is biographical in a way that the earlier essays on this author (in *La Part du feu*) had not been. The same mode of analysis is prolonged in a sequence of essays written in the 1950s and 1960s, which elaborate and qualify the statement of this first text, taking into account new material as it is published, and providing to an even greater degree the kind of documentation and informed supposition characteristic of biographical criticism. But *De Kafka à Kafka* also contains essays, such as 'The Narrative Voice' and 'The Wooden Bridge', both first collected in *L'Entretien infini*, which are in a quite different critical mode, and do not enter into biographical reflection. One can say then that the analysis of the literary experience represents one among other critical modes in Blanchot's writing.

For the sake of economy, we can refer to the text entitled 'La Folie par excellence', on Hölderlin, in order to illustrate the assumptions of this mode of criticism. This text was written at around the same time as the first of the studies that make up *L'Espace littéraire*, and deploys procedures of analysis that had not till that point been so marked, but which then become prevalent for a time. It is clearly divided into two relatively discrete sections. Here we are concerned with the first part, which responds to a psychiatric study of artistic creation by Karl Jaspers, dealing primarily with Van Gogh, but also Strindberg and Hölderlin.[20] Following the direction indicated by Jaspers, Blanchot reflects on the problems of interpretation raised by the intersecting trajectories of Hölderlin's mental illness (accessible to clinical analysis as schizophrenia) and that of his development as a poet (demanding an immanent reading). The essay is marked by an unusually tentative tone: it sketches out several possible angles of approach, but then each time arrests the inquiry, allowing that it does not gain access to the real problem. The general conclusions, however, are altogether categorical. Hölderlin's history, he suggests, cannot be adequately understood in terms of his particular temperament, nor purely in terms of his illness, since it is 'not his destiny but the poetic destiny that decides'.[21] There is, then, a definite and in principle general way of seeing the unfolding of the poetic phenomenon which, if it is not exactly an explanatory schema, like those of psychology or pathology, nonetheless can and should take their place in understanding literary works. Compare, for example, the beginning of the essay on Mallarmé in *L'Espace littéraire*, on the encounter with nothingness and with death, of which the poet writes in his

---

20 *Strindberg und Van Gogh: Versuch einer vergleichenden pathographischen Analyse*, Bircher, 1922. The second part is concerned directly with the interpretation of Hölderlin; we have considered it in our Chapter 2.
21 *'La folie par excellence'*, *Critique*, n° 45, 1951, 111–112.

Myth and Representation in Blanchot's Criticism   131

letters of 1867. These episodes, Blanchot stipulates, have '*nothing anecdotal*' about them; they issue from the concentration on the act of writing: 'writing appears as an extreme situation, which supposes a radical reversal' (EL 37, 38); during these years, the poetic task 'draws [Mallarmé] into an obscure experience, where he is essentially at risk' (EL 136, 108–109).

In reviewing the episodes of a literary life or the changing attitudes of writers in relation to their work, Blanchot always moves to distance the various known and recognizable schemes by which such material could be interpreted, and points instead in the direction of something like a 'poetic destiny' or a 'poetic demand'. The obsessive component in writing, the inability to finish, the literary breakdowns, renunciations and suicides are not to be understood in terms of the individual psychology: nor are they to be seen socio-historically, in terms, for example, of the growing separation between artist and audience characteristic of the nineteenth and twentieth centuries (to indicate an alternative possible orientation). Instead, they appear as the signs and traces of the encounter with the very possibility of literary writing. This premise, first formulated as such in this text on Hölderlin, becomes a formal thesis in *L'Espace littéraire*:

> The work attracts the one who devotes himself to it to the point at which it encounters its own impossibility ('*L'oeuvre attire celui qui s'y consacre vers le point où elle est à l'épreuve de son impossibilité*'). (EL 105, 213: 87, 163)

In such sentences, Blanchot gives hermetically condensed expression to the understanding that has emerged from the preceding philosophical and critical reflection.[22] 'The point at which the work encounters its impossibility' is without doubt what has elsewhere been presented as the experience of 'essential solitude', the encounter with the 'he' that doubles and dispossesses the subject (cf. our Chapter 4). 'The

---

22 In another such formulation, this 'point' is not only the centre but also 'the origin' of the work: 'The work tends towards its origin, to the centre at which it will be able to be completed. In the search for this point the work is progressively realized, but when it is attained, it makes the work impossible' ('*L'oeuvre tend vers son origine, ce centre où seulement elle pourra s'accomplir, dans la recherche duquel elle se réalise et qui, atteint, la rend impossible*') (EL 97, 81).

one who devotes himself to [the work]' does so *as* a self, entering into writing by a free decision, commencing the work with the same basic attitude and expectations as any other project. For Blanchot, however, the act of writing is not a movement from idea to realization, but only begins with the 'leap' from action in the world and the time of work to the experience of solitude, fascination and repetition ('the leap is the form or the movement of inspiration', EL 232, 177). The access to space of the work is experienced as an exile from the horizon of the future, from the shape and the sense of an activity given by its relation to an end. The term 'attraction' suggests that this transition is approached in a kind of semi-consciousness, neither as willed action nor pure determination, but in the passive–active mode of being that is also evoked by a number of other terms, such as 'fascination' or, in later texts, *la veille*.

In the observation of this movement in writers, Blanchot's hermeneutic 'style' has something of a clinical aspect. This does not necessarily signify that it is a method that is indifferently applied to any given text (which would be an unduly reductive view of the diagnostic activity, in any case). It does mean, however, that this criticism is informed by an awareness of characteristic signs, typical reactions and phases, illustrating the possible variations upon a central underlying phenomenon. To the extent that this reaction and response only becomes explicit for the analyst, not for the writer, the structure is similar to that of the psychoanalytic claim to uncover an unconscious motivation. This similarity is visible above all in the quasi-fictive narrations of the writer's experience, dramatizing the writer's movement as a dream-like fascination, drawing him out of himself with the inevitability of an unfolding fate. The situation is a little different, however, once we move from statements about 'the writer' in general to the critical texts on Hölderlin, Mallarmé and Kafka. Here it is not a matter of illustrating an impersonal law, but of reconstructing the history of an understanding. The interpretation tracks the paths by which each of these writers discovers that the privation of self and possibility is implicated in the literary activity itself (and is therefore not merely a consequence, an effect or a symptom).

That there is such a consciousness and that it has an historical significance is stated with the greatest directness in the text entitled 'Inspiration, Lack of Inspiration' (EL V.iii). In the past, Blanchot writes, the encounter with impossibility, with the absence of time, was mediated by categories that allowed works to pass through it, without recognizing it (such as 'inspiration', one can suppose). Now, however, the work is 'no longer innocent, it knows where it comes from' (EL 245–246, 186). Modern literature, for Blanchot, is the history of an every closer approach to its origin. The result, as Blanchot argues in 'The Search for the Zero Point', is the dispersion of forms and genres, the dissolution of conventions of character, place and meaning, and ultimately the separation of literature and the self, as the pressure of the search pushes writing to the point at which all that speaks is an 'impersonal neutrality' (LV 272, 200). The same movement appears at the level of the individual history in many of the studies of individual writers. Kafka 'sees always more clearly that he belongs to the other side' (*l'autre rive*), recognizes ever more clearly that what the work demands of him is that he learn to 'occupy' the outside (EL 91, 76). In the essay on Rilke: 'After having at first seen in art "a path towards myself" [Rilke] recognizes ever more that this path has to lead to the point where, in myself, I belong to the outside, that it leads me there where I am no longer myself, where, if I speak, it is not me who speaks, where I cannot speak' (EL 203–204, 155–156). And Mallarmé, tormented by sterility, 'recognizes that this deprivation is not a mere personal failing, but that it announces the encounter with the work, the menacing intimacy of this encounter' (EL 233, 177).

At first sight, it may seem that what is being discovered here is an unequivocally negative predicament: with more or less lucidity, each writer comes to recognize the force of dispossession, the attraction of the 'outside', concealed within the demand of art and literature. But this summary, as accurate as it seems, misrepresents the orientation of the interpretation. In order to see this point, however, one has to recognize the philosophical significance of the experience of 'impossibility'. This really only becomes explicit in *L'Entretien infini*, when Blanchot proposes that this term can be understood in a sense that is no longer governed by the category of possibility: impossibility, then, is not failure as a modification of possibility, or the negation that is at its limit (EI 61–64, 43–45). The experience of 'impossibility' – which is then used to encompass all that is developed in earlier texts as solitude, exile, error – is not conceived as a phenomenon of deficiency, an abyss beneath our existence into which we risk to fall. It is an original dimension of our existence, given to us with the opening of possibility. From the moment at which we encounter things in the mode of possibility, from the moment that we affirm ourselves as a power in the world, we are exposed to the inertia of absence, the power of recommencement, the incessant and the interminable. The 'neutrality' that Blanchot associates with this moment signifies that it has nothing to do with the person who we are, and yet, because in order to be ourselves we have drawn on the resources of negation, we also continue to belong to the space of the outside in the mode of 'impossibility'.[23] Accordingly, the passivity, the inertia towards which the movement of literature draws the writer, is not solely to be interpreted as the dissolution of the self that would be 'caused' by some property of writing (its fictionality, for example, or the solitude in which it is carried out, its disconnect from a utilitarian society, etc.). What is discovered in modern literature is not any kind of negative consequence, but, on the contrary, a certain kind of 'possibility' – provided that we hear this word in a sense that is not commanded by the experience of power and possibility proper to the self in the world. A passage from 'Inspiration, Lack of Inspiration' (EL V.iii), again deploying the motif of attraction in order to dramatize the writer's situation (here, in the form of the 'we'), can serve to illustrate how this is the case. In writing, Blanchot proposes:

> We are attracted, by a too powerful movement, into a space where truth is absent, where the limits have disappeared, a space without measure, and yet it is there that it is required that we remain on the path (*il nous est imposé de maintenir une démarche juste*), not to lose the measure, and to seek a true speech (*une parole vraie*) in going to the end of error. (243, 184)

To remain on the path, to maintain the measure, to go to the end of error, to bind ourselves to the non-true – these expressions designate what we can only call (for lack of better terms) a form of possibility, even the prospect of an accomplishment. It is the same possibility that is mapped out by the whole linguistic complex associated with writing in Blanchot's text – in terms such as belonging and hearing, adapted from Heidegger, as well as in a series of motifs proper to

---

23 Cf. Chapter 4, Section iii.

Blanchot, such as patience and impatience, or attraction and negligence.[24] Through the exposition of the dimensions of 'impossibility' Blanchot shows us that we can begin to read modern literary history outside of the conceptual space dictated by the modern age from which it emerges, which is to say, effectively, no longer to understand it as a kind of work on social meanings or, alternately, on an autonomous formal language. The initial historical position and the assumptions it commands is bound to determine the sense of what it is that is valued under the literary, and hence to provide the parameters and the limits of its understanding.

---

24 Our references here are to the language of *L'Espace littéraire*, but this same possibility that is pursued in later texts, under different forms, as *'la parole du détour'*, for example, in *'Parler, ce n'est pas voir'*; cf. EI 42–45, 30–32.

Reprise: Blanchot and Literary Criticism

This study has emphasized the historical dimension of Blanchot's criticism. There are also other, relatively independent areas of critical interest that have been little touched upon here. Much could be done, for example, on the treatment of literary genres or modes, such as the novel, the *récit*, the diary, the fragment. The approach chosen has the advantage, however, that it allows one to see how Blanchot's essays can be inscribed within the horizon of a project which could in principle be the topic of research and debate within the discipline of literary studies.

In Blanchot, the operative historical categories are understood in philosophical terms, and not in reference to empirical and chronological coordinates. Following philosophical–historical guidelines established by Hegel and Heidegger, modernity is understood as the age of subjectivity, of reason as power and as will to power. This historical interpretation is taken over and restated in Blanchot's own conceptuality: the modern age is that in which 'nothingness becomes a power' and in which, in consequence, 'man is fully historical' (EL 339, 252 cf. Chapter 4). The consolidation of the thought of the epoch around the subject, and the preeminence of the values of power and domination compels those who devote themselves to literature and art to confront these instances as minor forms of power, and this marginalization, as we have seen, creates the conditions for a revaluation of the sense and possibility of literature and art. In Blanchot's representation, modern literature and art are characterized, in their most general traits, by a new sense of the possibility and the enigma represented by their own being, as well as a dissatisfaction with the forms and values with which they have come to be identified. 'Modern' literature is not merely the production of 'new' poems, novels and paintings, of works that in their style or meaning are appreciably different from those that have appeared before: the modern work is the one that is concerned with its own possibility whose 'subject' is its own accomplishment (cf. our Chapter 1).

In studying Blanchot's essays *as* criticism, it becomes apparent that they are conditioned in all of their aspects – in the choice of texts, the identification of salient historical features, the direction of the readings – by a philosophical position that is elaborated within and alongside the properly critical work of his texts. The critical and the philosophical dimensions of the work are intimately intertwined, to the point where, in reading the work, one does not have a strong sense of a qualitative difference between the studies of particular authors and the texts in which Blanchot advances his own poetics. For this reason, too, the critical conclusions cannot be assessed through direct comparison with existing interpretations of the same author, but would first demand a decision on the philosophical claims.

The direction of the thought, at least, seems to be formed already in some of the earliest works. In 'From Anguish to Language', the rather abstract and monological reflection that opens *Faux Pas*, Blanchot's first collection of critical essays, literary writing is said to be made possible by a 'fundamental anxiety', and by the 'nothing' that this anxiety reveals to the writer (FP 9–15, 4–13). This line of thought is continued in *La Part du feu*, in a series of paradoxical and negative declarations: 'what makes language possible is that it tends to be impossible' (PF 30, 22): writing begins with 'a certain incapacity to speak, and to write, with the absence of the very means that [the writer] has to excess. Thus it is indispensable that he feel at first that he has nothing to say' (PF 74, 69), and still in *L'Espace littéraire*: 'writing could only have its origin in the "true" despair, the one that leads one to nothing, and first of all withdraws the pen from the writer' (EL 63, 57). Through the repetition and the restatement of the intuition condensed in these paradoxes, Blanchot's thought unfolds and finds its path. The series of texts on Mallarmé in *La Part du feu* would count among the decisive stages on this path. For Blanchot, Mallarmé is the paradigmatic modern poet: his work is marked by the transition from the composition of a series of discrete poems to the 'concern by which the work becomes the search for its origin, and wants to identify itself with its origin, *"vision horrible d'une oeuvre pure"'* (EL 43, 42). The treatment of Mallarmé shows well the characteristic ambiguity of Blanchot's critical procedure. At the literary–historical level, his works stands as a verification of the thesis that modern poetry is animated by the concern for its own possibility. On the exegetic level, Blanchot's study provides a sketch of an integral reading of the work, organizing the language and the movement of Mallarmé's poetry around the experience of 'absence' and 'silence' as the origin of the poetic act. But when in the essays that follow, Mallarmé's work is taken to represent the poetic as such becoming conscious of itself, and as exhibiting a motivation present in all poetry (PF 69–70, 64–65), then one sees that the argument depends upon a prior 'knowledge' of poetry, which is necessary in order to see what is discovered in the work of Mallarmé.

For all the freedom with which the text moves to the essential, however, one could not conclude that it simply imposes an *a priori* schema upon the poetic text. On the contrary, the line of influence also goes in the other direction, and the reading of Mallarmé in *La Part du feu* marks the beginning of a reflection on the relation between language, absence and silence, which will continue to resonate throughout Blanchot's work. Such an interplay is visible, to varying degrees, in all of these studies: there is not a clear separation between the critical method and assumptions and the interpretive conclusions that are supposed, by the normal understanding, to result from the application of the model.

One can see, however, that the relatively autonomous recasting of the problematic in certain texts has a decisive impact on the terms of the inquiry. 'Literature and the Right to Death' is a key text, since it gathers together the elements of a philosophical thought that emerges intermittently in the course of *La Part du feu*. In this text, we see that the power over the world that language opens up to us has its ground in an initial relation to absence, drawn from our anticipated relation to death. The exercise of this power, however, requires us to overlook the other 'face' of death, under which it appears, not as a source of power and distance in relation to the world, but as the deprivation of all possibility, and even of the 'right to death'. Literature, it is claimed, has its origin in this ambiguity of the negative. Henceforth, this becomes the sense of the 'possibility' of speaking and writing in which, from the earliest texts, Blanchot had affirmed that writing and literature have their 'origin' – the paradox now signifying that writing does not belong to possibility, as a name for the total dimension of existence, opened by the possession (in idea) of death.

This clarification sets the agenda for *L'Espace littéraire*, as a fundamental representation of the literary work and the literary experience, taking its 'foundation' in the ambiguity of the negative. On this premise, all notions of the literary that take their bearing from the scheme of work and production are refused. Literary writing and literary reading are not the exercise of a power, essentially like other forms of power, qualified only by the fact that they operate in the realm of language and images. The literary work does not have the reality of a cultural object or a 'text': it exists only as the demand of a leap, into which one has to enter in abandoning the security of the world. Writing is only possible if the writer approaches the point at which language is no longer a power, at which it is only its image, an imaginary language (EL 51, 48); the writer has to belong to fascination and experiences the solitude in which the I becomes no one, has to live the absence of time, to dwell in the outside, where nothing ever begins, where the reality of events dissolves into their indefinite repetition (EL I–III); and the reader has to become the impersonal consent that allows the work to affirm itself, apart from all relations of power and knowledge (EL VI).

This standpoint and this language permeate the reading of particular literary works. In some texts (such as those on Hölderlin), the themes and the figures of individual works are taken over for a reflection on the historical sense and the possibility of poetry. Many texts are interested in the writer's relation to his work, as manifested in diaries, in letters, in biographical details: the approach to the work is traced through the partial discoveries, the hesitations and false steps, the paths retraced or avoided, the sudden *dénouements* and the interminable prolongations. At points, the studies critically engage with the writer's own reflective or programmatic statements on writing and literature, separating out precipitate conclusions or theoretical rationalizations from what is most revealing in their experience, and following the way the latter gradually imposes itself. We see this pattern, for example, in the long central section of *L'Espace littéraire*, exploring the relations of poetry and death in Mallarmé and Rilke.

The critical 'work' of these texts, then, requires the understanding of the poetic that appears in *L'Espace littéraire* alongside the studies. One can say that this conception allows texts to be seen in a way in which they otherwise would not, but these observations are not advanced as evidence for the general statements on the poetic. In order to assess the validity of Blanchot's work as criticism, what needs to be decided is the *status* of the underlying assumptions and their relation to the critical statements that they generate. The support that is found in

Heidegger's thought in *L'Espace littéraire* helps to see the problems involved. In its style and procedures, Blanchot's criticism is not especially similar to Heidegger's own work on poetry. It is not for the most part exegetic, as are Heidegger's readings of Hölderlin and of other poets. The relation to 'the outside', engaged in writing, provides a projection, within and against which, it seems, the work of nearly any writer can be considered: the conceptuality of negativity seems to allow for greater generality than the thought of being, and hence for something closer to a critical practice. But the interpretations are situated at a similar distance from knowledge; in each case, the conceptuality with which they come to the work is not theoretical, but rather philosophical, thinking art in terms of its foundation in language and existence, not in terms of the definition of the literary, by its linguistic properties or its cultural and institutional status. This means that much of what has been said about the legitimacy from the critical point of view of Heidegger's studies of poetry would be transferable to Blanchot's work. Nearly all the critics who deal with this question in the case of Heidegger have inclined towards a negative verdict. It is true that this question has often been taken up from a standpoint that is openly negative, and even hostile, towards Heidegger's entire enterprise. It has been little explored from within the fold of Heideggerean scholarship, perhaps because the question of legitimacy in the terms of the epistemology of the human sciences does not pose itself for a thinking and a writing which aims to occupy and to work within the space opened by Heidegger's thought. Hence the interest of the recent work by Appelhans, which, in great detail and without animosity, makes the case that the criteria of interpretive argument are not sustained by Heidegger's discourse, that its conclusions are entirely programmed by its assumptions, and that they are not verifiable by textual evidence.[1]

If these conclusions are correct, and the extension is valid, then Blanchot's work would seem to diverge irreconcilably from literary criticism. The critical content in Blanchot would have validity only in this text, for a thinking and a writing that already stands in relation to 'the outside'. This conclusion, of course, also suggests the

---

1 Jörg Appelhans, *Heideggers ungeschriebene Poetologie*. Tübingen: Niemayer, 2002.

possibility that the horizon of correct or defensible interpretation is sustained by its own presuppositions. Precisely because of the problems that it raises concerning the prior horizon of understanding, the Heideggerean type approach invites criticism to theorize the 'inside' from which it interprets and validates interpretation.

We can gain some perspective here by stepping back to less imposing questions of value and attitude. On this level, with respect to modern literature, the results are strikingly different, depending on which of the two starting points one takes, the critical–disciplinary or that of Blanchot. The latter seems to take modern literature more seriously and to see it more positively than literary criticism generally does, at least at the present time. Throughout his studies of individual writers, Blanchot grants a certain legitimacy to the transformations of modern literature, and inscribes his own thinking as the continuation of its movement. This is something to which the criticism of the last 30 years has been very little inclined. Instead, the passion for literature, the claim for it as an absolute, is seen as a substitute for (or a 'secularization' of) the kind of affirmations that had been made by religion in the past; or the uniqueness of the literary work is seen as a means of preserving the experience of the individual against the indifference of a scientific epistemology; or again the emergence of a difficult literature, intended for a select readership, is seen as the restoration of caste distinctions on another plane, through the production of a spiritual elite. No doubt some of these threads are also present in the 'search for art', but the force of the critiques is diminished if there is not any position within the discourse from which it can be allowed that there is something valid or original in the phenomenon. It may be that the assimilation of the thought of being – which does allow it validity and originality – would make demands that are too great on the institutions of knowledge and on discourse, requiring these instances to cross the barrier that, for all the diversity of approaches in literary criticism, rules out anything which, from their standpoint, can only be named as 'metaphysics'. And yet it may also be that this interdict has been transgressed from the beginning, with the supposition that there could be something such as 'literary criticism' or 'literary studies'. One can wonder to what extent this discipline owes its essential assumption – that one can read and study texts as literary – to the resonance of the affirmations of modern literature, rather than to any theoretically founded methodological conception. If this is true, then in reading Blanchot, and in thinking about the relation of his work to knowledge, literary criticism is offered a path by which it can approach its own origins, and decide again its own possibility.

Selected Bibliography

Works of Maurice Blanchot

A number of Blanchot's books have been re-published in more commonly available paperback editions, and it is these that are cited below. The initial publication year follows in parentheses, if different. This listing is confined to Blanchot's works of literary criticism and philosophy.

Faux Pas. Paris: Gallimard, 1943.
La Part du feu. Paris: Gallimard, 1949.
Lautréamont et Sade. Second edition with new preface. Paris: Minuit, 1963 (first published, 1949).
'La Folie par excellence.' *Critique*, n° 45, February 1951, 99–118. This is the sole uncollected essay from this period which is not reprinted (for copyright reasons) in the recent collection edited by Christophe Bident, entitled *La Condition critique* (see below).
L'Espace littéraire. Paris: Gallimard (Folio essais), 1988 (first published, 1955).
Le Livre à venir. Paris: Gallimard (Folio essais), 1986 (first published, 1959).
L'Entretien infini. Paris: Gallimard, 1969.
L'Amitié. Paris: Gallimard, 1971.
Le Pas au-delà. Paris: Gallimard, 1973.
L'Écriture du désastre. Paris: Gallimard, 1980.
Après Coup, précédé par le ressassement éternel. Paris: Minuit, 1983.
De Kafka à Kafka. Paris: Gallimard (Folio essais), 1994 (first published, 1981).
Une Voix venue d'ailleurs. Paris: Gallimard (Folio essais), 2002.
Chroniques Littéraires du journal des débats: avril 1941–août 1944. Ed. Christophe Bident. Paris: Gallimard (Cahiers de la NRF), 2007.
La Condition critique: articles 1945–1998. Ed. Christophe Bident. Paris: Gallimard (Cahiers de la NRF), 2010.

English Translations

The English translations are listed corresponding to the order of their initial French publication, as given above.
The Book to Come. Trans. Charlotte Mandell. Stanford: Stanford UP, 2003.

Faux Pas. Trans. Charlotte Mandell. Stanford: Stanford UP, 2001.
Friendship. Trans. Elizabeth Rottenberg. Stanford: Stanford UP, 1997.
The Infinite Conversation. Trans. Susan Hanson. Minneapolis: University of Minnesota Press, 1993.
Lautréamont and Sade. Trans. Stuart Kendall and Michelle Kendall. Stanford: Stanford UP, 2004.
The Space of Literature. Trans. Ann Smock. Lincoln: University of Nebraska Press, 1982.
The Step Not Beyond. Trans. Lycette Nelson. Albany: State University of New York Press, 1992.
A Voice from Elsewhere. Trans. Charlotte Mandell. Albany: State University of New York Press, 2007.
The Work of Fire. Trans. Charlotte Mandell. Stanford: Stanford UP, 1995.
The Writing of the Disaster. Trans. Ann Smock. Lincoln: University of Nebraska Press, 1986.

The following books translate selections of essays from different collections and periods:

The Blanchot Reader. Ed. Michael Holland. Oxford: Blackwell, 1995.
The Sirens' Song. Trans. Sacha Rabinovitch. Brighton: Harvester, 1982.
The Station Hill Blanchot Reader. Ed. George Quasha. New York: Station Hill Press, 1998.

Selected Bibliography

This bibliography is confined to studies relevant to the works of Blanchot and to topics treated in this book. Where available, references are to works in English translation; the reference to the original is given only when it has been cited in the text.

Abrams, M. H. 'Coleridge, Baudelaire and Modernist Poetics.' *The Correspondent Breeze: Essays on English Romanticism.* New York: Norton, 1984, 109–144.

Agamben, Georgio. *Language and Death: The Place of Negativity.* Trans. Karen E. Pinkus. Minneapolis: University of Minnesota Press, 1991.

Appelhans, Jörg. *Heideggers Ungeschriebene Poetologie.* Tübingen: Niemayer, 2002.

Balfour, Ian. *The Rhetoric of Romantic Prophecy.* Stanford: Stanford UP, 2002.

Barthes, Roland. *Writing Degree Zero and Elements of Semiology.* Trans. Annette Lavers and Colin Smith. London: Jonathan Cape, 1984.

Bataille, Georges. *Guilty.* Trans. Bruce Boone. Venice, CA: Lapis Press, 1988.

———. *Inner Experience.* Trans. Leslie Anne Boldt. Albany: SUNY Press, 1988.

———. *On Nietzsche.* Trans. Bruce Boone. New York: Paragon House, 1992.

Bénichou, Paul. *Selon Mallarmé.* Paris: Gallimard, 1995.

Robert Bernasconi and Simon Critchley (eds) *Re-reading Levinas*. Bloomington: Indiana UP, 1991.
Bident, Christophe. *Maurice Blanchot: partenaire invisible*. Paris: Champ Vallon, 1998.
Binder, Wolfgang. *Hölderlin Aufsätze*. Frankfurt: Insel, 1970.
Blumenberg, Hans. *The Legitimacy of the Modern Age*. Trans. Robert Wallace. Cambridge, MA: MIT Press, 1983.
Bruns, Gerald L. *Maurice Blanchot and the Refusal of Philosophy*. Baltimore: Johns Hopkins UP, 1997.
Butler, Judith. *Subjects of Desire: Hegelian Reflections in Twentieth-Century France*. New York: Columbia UP, 1987.
Cassirer, Ernst. *The Philosophy of the Enlightenment*. Trans. Fritz Koelln and James Pettegrove. Princeton: Princeton UP, 1951.
Clark, Timothy. 'Blanchot's Contradictory Passion: Inspiration in *The Space of Literature*', *SubStance*, vol. 25, no. 1, 1996, 46–61.
Critchley, Simon. *Very Little – Almost Nothing: Death, Philosophy, Literature*. London: Routledge, 1997.
Dambre, Marc and Gosselin-Noat, Monique (eds). *L'Éclatement des genres au vingtième siècle*. Paris: Presse de la Sorbonne Nouvelle, 2001.
De Man, Paul. *Blindness and Insight: Essays in the Rhetoric of Contemporary Criticism*. Second revised edition. London: Methuen, 1983.
———. *Critical Writings: 1953–1978*. Ed. Lindsay Waters. Minneapolis: University of Minnesota Press, 1989.
Derrida, Jacques. *L'Écriture et la différence*. Paris: Éditions du Seuil, 1967.
———. *Parages*. Paris: Galilée, 1986.
———. *Demeure: Maurice Blanchot*. Paris: Galilée, 1988.
Descombes, Vincent. *Modern French Philosophy*. Trans. L. Scott-Fox and J.M. Harding. Cambridge UP, 1980.
Durand, Pascal. *Poésies de Stéphane Mallarmé*. Paris: Gallimard, 1998.
Foucault, Michel. 'Maurice Blanchot, the Thought from Outside'. Trans. Brian Massumi, in *Foucault/Blanchot*. New York: Zone, 1987, 7–60.
Frow, John. *Genre*. New York: Routledge, 2005.
Fynsk, Christopher. *Language and Relation . . . that there is language*. Stanford: Stanford UP, 1996.
Gasché, Rodolphe. *Of Minimal Things: Studies in the Notion of Relation*. Stanford: Stanford UP, 1999.
Graff, Gerald. *Professing Literature: An Institutional History*. Chicago: University of Chicago Press, 1987.
Gregg, John. *Maurice Blanchot and the Literature of Transgression*. Princeton: Princeton UP, 1994.
Guerlac, Suzanne. *Literary Polemics: Bataille, Sartre, Valéry, Breton*. Stanford: Stanford UP, 1997.
Habermas, Jürgen. *The Philosophical Discourse of Modernity*. Trans. Frederick G. Lawrence. Cambridge, MA: MIT Press, 1987.

146 Selected Bibliography

Harlingue, Oliver. *Sans Condition: Blanchot, la litterature, la philosophie.* Paris: Harmattan, 2009.
Harries, Karsten and Jammes, Christophe (eds). *Martin Heidegger: Politics, Art and Technology.* New York: Holmes and Meier, 1994.
Hart, Kevin. *The Dark Gaze: Maurice Blanchot and the Sacred.* Chicago: University of Chicago Press, 2004.
Hegel, G. W. F. *Aesthetics: Lectures on Fine Art.* Trans. T. M. Knox. Oxford: Clarendon Press, 1975.
——. *Hegel's Preface to the Phenomenology of Spirit.* Translated and commentary by Yirmiyahu Yovel. Princeton, NJ: Princeton University Press, 2005.
——. *Introduction to the Philosophy of History.* Trans. Leo Rauch. Indianapolis: Hackett, 1988.
Heidegger, Martin. *Being and Time.* Trans. John Macquarie and Edward Robinson. NY: Harper and Row, 1962.
——. *Einführung in die Metaphysik.* Tübingen: Niemeyer, 1998.
——. *Einleitung zur Philosophie (Gesamtausgabe*, vol. 27). Frankfurt: Klostermann, 2001.
——. *Elucidations of Hölderlin's Poetry.* Trans. Keith Hoeller. Amherst, NY: Humanity Books, 2000.
——. *Erläuterungen zu Hölderlins Dichtung.* Frankfurt: Klostermann, 1951.
——. *Holzwege.* Frankfurt: Klostermann, 1976.
——. *Off the Beaten Track.* Trans. Julian Young and Kenneth Haynes. NY: Cambridge University Press, 2002.
——. *Pathmarks.* Ed. William McNeil. Cambridge: Cambridge UP, 1998.
——. *Sein und Zeit.* Eleventh edition. Tubingen: Niemeyer, 1967.
——. *Vorträge und Aufsätze.* Pfullingen: Günther Neske, 1954.
——. *Was heisst Denken.* Tübingen: Niemeyer, 1954.
——. *Wegmarken.* Frankfurt: Klostermann, 1996.
Herrmann, Wilhelm Friedrich von. *Wahrheit, Freiheit, Geschichte.* Frankfurt: Klostermann, 1992.
——. *Heideggers Philosophie der Kunst: eine systematische Interpretation der Holzwege-Abhandlung 'Der Ursprung des Kunstwerks'.* Frankfurt: Klostermann, 1980.
Hill, Leslie. *Bataille, Klossowski, Blanchot: Writing at the Limit.* New York: Oxford UP, 2001.
——. *Blanchot: Extreme Contemporary.* London: Routledge, 1997.
Hölderlin, Friedrich. *Sämtliche Werke.* Six volumes. Ed. Friedrich Beissner. Stuttgart: J.G. Cottache, 1948–1985.
Hyppolite, Jean. *Studies on Marx and Hegel.* Trans. John O'Neill. London: Heinemann, 1969.
Iyer, Lars. *Blanchot's Vigilance: Literature, Phenomenology and the Ethical.* New York: Palgrave MacMillan, 2005.
Jacobs, Carol. *Skirting the Ethical.* Stanford, CA: Stanford UP, 2008.

Janicaud, Dominique. *Heidegger en France*. Two volumes. Paris: Albin Michel, 2001.
Jaspers, Karl. *Strindberg und Van Gogh: Versuch einer vergleichenden pathographischen Analyse*. Leipzig: E. Bircher, 1922.
Kermode, Frank. *The Romantic Image*. London: Routledge, 1957.
Kojève, Alexander. *Introduction à la lecture de Hegel: leçons sur la phénoménologie de l'esprit*. Ed. Raymond Queneau. Paris: Gallimard, 1947.
Langan, Janine D. *Hegel and Mallarmé*. New York: University Press of America, 1986.
Large, William. 'Impersonal Existence: A Conceptual Genealogy of the "there is" from Heidegger to Blanchot and Levinas', *Angelaki*, vol. 7, no. 3, 2002, 131–142.
Levinas, Emmanuel. *De l'existence à l'existant*. Second Edition. Paris: Vrin, 1963 (first published, 1947).
——. *Discovering Existence with Heidegger and Husserl*. Trans. Richard Cohen and Michael Smith. Evanston, IL: Northwestern UP, 1998.
Limet, Yun Sun. *Maurice Blanchot critique*. Paris: Éditions de la Différence, 2010.
Löwith, Karl. *From Hegel to Nietzsche: The Revolution in Nineteenth-Century Thought*. Trans. David E. Green. London: Constable, 1964.
Mallarmé, Stephane. *Igitur, Divagations, Un Coup de dés*. Paris: Gallimard, 1976.
——. *Divagations: The Author's 1897 Arrangement; Together with 'Autobiography' and 'Music and Letters'*. Trans. Barbara Johnson. Cambridge, MA: Harvard UP, 2007.
Marchal, Bertrand. *Lire le symbolisme*. Paris: Dunod, 1993.
Mauron, Charles. *Mallarmé l'obscur*. Paris: Denöel, 1941.
McNeil, William. *The Glance of the Eye: Heidegger, Aristotle and the Ends of Theory*. Albany: SUNY Press, 1999.
Michel, Chantal. *Maurice Blanchot et le déplacement d'Orphée*. Saint-Genouph: Nizet, 1997.
Nordholt, Anne-Lise Schulte. *Maurice Blanchot: l'écriture comme expérience du dehors*. Geneva: Droz, 1995.
Paulhan, Jean. *The Flowers of Tarbes, or Terror in Literature*. Trans. Michael Syrotinski. Urbana: University of Illinois Press, 2006.
——. *On Poetry and Politics*. Trans. Jennifer Bajorek, Charlotte Mandell and Eric Trudel. Urbana: University of Illinois Press, 2008.
Poulet, Georges. *La Distance intérieure*. Paris: Plon, 1952.
Ricoeur, Paul. *Hermeneutics and the Human Sciences: Essays on Language, Action and Interpretation*. Trans. John. H. Thompson. New York: Cambridge UP, 1981.
Robbins, Jill. *Altered Reading: Levinas and Literature*. Chicago: University of Chicago Press, 1999.

Roth, Michael. *Knowing and History: Appropriations of Hegel in Twentieth-Century France*. Ithaca: Cornell UP, 1988.
Sallis, John. *Double Truth*. Albany, NY: SUNY Press, 1995.
Sartre, Jean-Paul. *The Imaginary: A Phenomenological Psychology of the Imagination*. Trans. Jonathan Webber. London and New York: Routledge, 2004.
——. *Being and Nothingness: An Essay on Phenomenological Ontology*. Trans. Hazel Barnes. London: Methuen, 1957.
——. *What Is Literature?* Trans. Bernard Frechtman. London: Routledge, 2005.
Schaeffer, Jean-Marie. *The Art of the Modern Age*. Trans. Steven Randall. Princeton, NJ: Princeton UP, 2000.
Schmidt, Jochen (ed.). *Über Hölderlin*. Frankfurt: Insel, 1970.
Schwartz, Sanford. *The Matrix of Modernism: Pound, Eliot and Early Twentieth-Century Thought*. Princeton, NJ: Princeton UP, 1985.
Schwarz, Stephen. 'Faux Pas: Maurice Blanchot and the Ontology of Literature', *SubStance*, vol. 27, no. 1, 1998, 19–47.
Swenson, James. 'Revolutionary Sentences', *Yale French Studies*, vol. 93, 1998, 11–28.
Taminiaux, Jacques. *Art et événement: spéculation et jugement des Grecs à Heidegger*. Paris: Belin, 2005.
——. *Poetry, Speculation and Judgment*. Trans. Michael Gendre. Albany: SUNY Press, 1993.
Todorov, Tzvetan. *Critique de la critique*. Paris: Éditions du Seuil, 1984.
——. *Genres in Discourse*. Trans. Catherine Porter. Cambridge: Cambridge UP, 1990.
Valéry, Paul. *Œuvres*. Two volumes. Paris: Gallimard, 1957.
Zarader, Marlène. *L'Être et le neutre: à partir de Maurice Blanchot*. Paris: Verdier, 2001.
Zima, Peter V. *The Philosophy of Modern Literary Theory*. London: Athlone, 1999.

Index

Words that have particular terminological value in Blanchot or that pose difficulties of translation are also given in French.

aesthetic autonomy 5–6, 40, 44, 53–4, 57
ambiguity xviii, 77–80, 88, 91–2, 99, 102, 138
anxiety (*l'angoisse*) 78, 86, 137

Bataille, Georges xix, 66, 71
beginning (*commencement*) xv, 27–9, 55, 123, 125–6

Char, René 12, 23, 102, 124
communication (*la communication*) xi, 108, 124
contestation (*la contestation*) 11, 16, 123–4

death xviii, 74, 77–8, 90–102, 121–2, 129, 134, 138
De Man, Paul ix–x
dissimulation (*la dissimulation*) xi, 30, 57–8, 61–2, 87–9, 94, 102, 115, 125
Dostoyevsky, Fyodor 96–9

error (*l'erreur*) 25, 33–5, 99–100, 128, 133–4

fascination (*la fascination*) 89, 99, 128–9, 132
Foucault, Michel 75–6

he (*il*) 89, 91, 100–1, 126, 131
Hegel, Georg Wilhelm Friedrich xiii, 2–8, 19, 40, 66, 68–71, 77, 83–5, 90, 96, 136

Heidegger, Martin xi, xiii–iv, xviii–xx, 21, 26–7, 43, 58–64, 70–3, 75–6, 82–3, 87–8, 91–4, 96, 99, 110–18, 121–2, 127–8, 134, 136, 140–1
Hofmannstahl, Hugo von 11–12, 121
Hölderlin, Friedrich xiii–xvi, xviii, 13, 18, 21–36, 43, 64, 68, 104, 120, 130–2, 139–40

the image viii, 20, 50, 101, 121, 126, 139
impossibility 22–3, 79, 89, 100, 124–6, 131–5, 137–8
inertia (*le désoeuvrement*) 33, 89, 101–2, 119, 121, 123, 126, 134
inspiration 81, 120, 132–4

Kafka, Franz 9, 13, 79, 87, 120–1, 129–30, 132–3
Kojève, Alexandre xiii, 3, 66, 69, 71, 83–4, 96

the leap (*le saut*) 100–1, 126, 132, 139
Levinas, Emmanuel xi, xix, 77, 87
the light (*le jour*) 5, 26–9, 70–1, 76, 91
literary criticism viii–xii, xx, 5, 12, 21, 31–2, 36, 44, 56, 64, 66, 69, 103, 105, 108, 116, 125, 127, 136, 139–42
literary theory viii, xiv, xviii, 16, 44, 104–5, 108–9, 123, 127, 140

Mallarmé, Stéphane xiii, xv–xviii, 9, 13, 17–18, 37–65, 66, 68, 73, 103–4, 110, 130–3, 137, 139

Index

modernity xiii, 2–8, 10, 19–20, 32, 35, 85, 88, 95, 96, 98, 135–6
modern literature xiii–xviii, xx, 1–2, 9–12, 15–20, 38–9, 66, 69, 105, 133–5, 137–8

negation 46, 69–70, 75, 77, 79, 83, 85, 89, 90, 134

the obscure (*l'obscur*) xi, 28–9, 125
the open 27, 61–3, 71, 112–13, 115
the outside (*le dehors*) 20, 99, 133, 139–40

Paulhan, Jean xix, 55, 104
possibility 89–91, 98–100, 102, 123, 132–4
Proust, Marcel 18, 129

reading xviii, 23, 109–10, 116, 123–6, 128

Rilke, Rainer Maria 9, 11–12, 53, 133, 139

the sacred 26–8, 36, 64
Sartre, Jean-Paul xi, xiii, xix, 66, 71, 86, 109
solitude xi, xv, 25–6, 33–4, 86–7, 107, 128–9, 131–4, 139

transcendence 72, 76, 102, 113–14

Valéry, Paul 11–12, 16, 39, 42, 53–4

the work (*l'oeuvre*) xi, xvi–xviii, 19, 37–8, 47, 54–8, 62–3, 100–1, 103–11, 114–16, 123–5, 127–8, 131, 139
writing xvi, xviii, 23, 110, 119–23, 125–6, 128–35

www.ingramcontent.com/pod-product-compliance
Lightning Source LLC
Chambersburg PA
CBHW052128300426
44116CB00010B/1810